A Neighborhood Café

A Guide and Celebration of Healthy Food and Community Engagement

Fran Ellen Weber

Solutions Press
Grass Valley, California

Illustrations by Donna Bishop
Photography by Philip Weber
Book design by Clarity Designworks

ISBN 979-8-9856110-0-7 (hardcover)
ISBN 979-8-9856110-1-4 (paperback, color interior)
ISBN 979-8-9856110-2-1 (paperback, black and white interior)
ISBN 979-8-9856110-3-8 (ebook)

Printed in the United States of America

This book is dedicated to my loving parents, Bernice and Gerry,
who gave me a healthy foundation from which to grow,
my son Danny, and Val, Ruby, and Jude.

To my late husband, Geoff, whose greatest passions in life
were found in knowledge, the solace of nature, and the gregariousness
of the "community of the table."

And, to my Aunt Sylvia, who has been a bright guiding light
for me throughout my life.

Contents

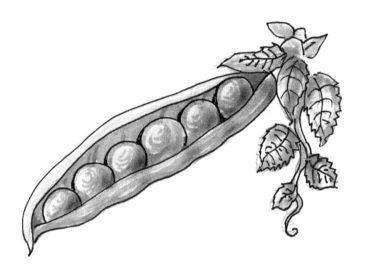

CHAPTER 1

An Introduction

The powerful effect of food on peoples' lives became apparent to me at an early age. I grew up in an easy-going, lower-middle-class Jewish household in Queens, New York, but my grandparents lived in a mixed Italian/Jewish neighborhood in Brooklyn. It was there that I experienced the importance that both cultures placed on food and family as their chief expressions of love. Family gatherings were generally spent around the dining-room table where we ate and conversed (often over one another), passionately expressing our differing opinions on life and politics. The evenings would typically end with warm hugs all around as we took those same convictions—little changed I suspect—home with us.

Home, for me, was a small cookie-cutter house in a new suburb between Kennedy and LaGuardia airports. My parents were able to purchase it, with help for a down payment from my dad's parents, for $17,000 in 1957. Whenever school friends from a different neighborhood came over to play, they would usually involuntarily duck every time a plane would fly close overhead. "How can you live here?" one such friend asked, and, being used to the sound and vibration, I responded quizzically, "What are you talking about?"

My dad would leave for his commute to work in Manhattan as an optician at 4 a.m. and typically return home by 7 p.m. During the 1960s that schedule was somewhat reversed when he worked nights at my mom's parents' luncheonette in Harlem, and temporarily at the post office during Christmas time.

In my sheltered suburb in Queens, I grew up attending primary school in an all-white, five-room wooden schoolhouse where I knew and loved both my teachers and classmates. After the city closed the building as a fire hazard, I was bussed and "subwayed" first to a large double-session junior high, and then a triple-session high school (until we moved closer to the latter). Both, as I remember, had a majority of black inner-city students. At the time, I felt outrage that I had lost the safety and love of my former school because of the inconvenient possibility that an outdated wooden schoolhouse might burn down one day. Why, I thought, didn't they just install more exit doors and hold more fire drills? Every morning I wished with all my heart that when I arrived at my new brick school I would find a pile of burnt rubble. This took place during the sixties, and the civil rights movement brought out much pent-up rage. I went to my new schools afraid every day.

Did I become prejudiced during those years of being part of a 40% minority? No. I feared the tough white girls as much as the black girls. I befriended both, occasionally more for reasons of safety than out of any genuine feelings of intimacy. I learned to never look anyone I didn't know in the eye to avoid the dreaded, "Who you lookin' at?" In a small way, I learned to identify with the stress and angst associated with being a minority, acutely aware that any day could bring trouble and harm because of what I looked like. And yet for those six years, I was able to go home after school each day to a safe environment, a luxury many minority populations can't enjoy. Years later, when living on my own in Manhattan, whenever I met the eyes of a black person and saw mistrust and anger in their stare, I would think to myself, "I know you got a raw deal; I'm not your enemy. I want things to change too!" In more recent times, when traveling through the south on one of my road trips to visit family in Pensacola, Florida, I thought those same words in silence as I watch many southern (especially elderly) African Americans walk with their eyes cast downward to avoid eye contact with me, a white stranger, a behavior, I presume, borne out of generational necessity and conditioning. Addressing and working towards changing these still existing conditions will benefit us all, and will strengthen and revitalize our nation.

I chose to leave city life to raise my son in, what was then, a sleepy little town in the Santa Cruz mountains of California, and I've become a country bumpkin at heart; I enjoy being part of a community. As my son Danny grew older, I loved that my fellow residents knew my son and had one eye out for him when I wasn't present. Yet I regret the lack of diversity that has marked these communities; the inability of small-town life to share the openness of big cities, characterized by the dizzying metropolitan mixture of religious, ethnic, color, and gender identities, has always struck me as the least satisfying aspect of small-town life. Many of the diverse relationships that I made during my teenage and young adult years have influenced me for the better; I've no doubt that this book grew out of these early friendships.

One such friendship provided me with one of my most cherished memories. During a "sleepover" at the home of a friend whose family had immigrated to New York from Greece, we awoke late Sunday morning to delicious kitchen aromas and considerable bustle. As my friend and I sat in the dining room, coffee in hand, the front doorbell rang. The first of many visitors had arrived, their food offerings graciously accepted and added to an already abundant array laid out on the dining room table. Every half hour or so, new guests would arrive and the routine was repeated. I lost count of how many new and delicious foods I tasted that day. Although people came and went throughout the afternoon, there always remained enough space for the newcomers to join us around the table. I didn't understand much of the conversation, since most of the family spoke their native Greek, but that didn't bother me at all. I drank in the love and laughter that filled the room, eating and laughing along with them, their joy infectious.

Food, love, and self-expression have always gone hand in hand for me. It's little wonder that I chose to become a chef when I graduated from high school in 1971. Yet when I received my Occupational Studies degree from the Culinary Institute of America in Hyde Park, New York, I was part of only the second graduating class to include female students.

During those years women were not yet accepted in professional kitchens, rarely considered hirable for much more than cold-pantry work (salads and cold appetizers) and the preparation and plating of cold desserts. While attending the Culinary Institute, I worked the graveyard shift at Dunkin' Donuts, behind the front counter because they wouldn't allow me in the kitchen to bake the donuts. One New Year's Eve, the manager got drunk in his office with a fellow female employee; he passed out, the baker called in sick, and I seized the moment. I baked the donuts for that particularly busy late night/early morning shift, and most of the employees and diners agreed that they came out better than usual, not a bit greasy and perfectly cooked. After proving myself (and bailing the manager out on New Year's Eve), he still refused to allow me to bake, so I gave notice and went elsewhere. After graduation, I would literally be laughed at during job interviews when I insisted that I wanted to cook, even though I had just graduated from one of the most prestigious culinary schools in the world: "You could never lift and carry a 50 lb. sack of onions" was a clichéd response to my persistence, but, indeed, I could do that. When I applied for a kitchen position at a fancy French restaurant in Manhattan, I was offered a job as a "hat check girl" instead. Finally, a country club north of the city hired me to work in the pantry, and I was determined to work my way up from there.

Early in my career, my hard work and schooling helped secure a promotion, awarded to me by an open-minded and extremely talented Swiss-German chef. He allowed me to move from the pantry of a large, busy seafood restaurant in Palm Beach, Florida, to the fry station on the hot cooking line. The fry station constitutes the bottom rung of the ladder on the cooking line, but "cooking, it was" and I was thrilled to have the opportunity. I reported to my new station the following day and, surprisingly, Chef Gerhardt was gone, replaced by an older, American career chef. I explained to my new boss why I was at the fry station ready to learn my new duties. He looked at me for what seemed quite a while and informed me that he "never had a female worker 'cook' in his kitchen, and I never will!" Of course, this occurred in the days when employers and managers could do and say many things without repercussions. Soon after, I joined Chef Gerhardt at his new post at an excellent Italian restaurant nearby. He became a treasured mentor to me, catapulting my career to a position that cushioned me from the full effects of gender prejudice in the culinary field.

One of the consequences of having to prove to myself and to others that I could do the same work as well as a man was the conviction that I had to do everything on my own, that I couldn't ask for help from my fellow male co-workers, even though they readily asked each other for help and would have happily helped me. I felt that asking for assistance would have suggested that I couldn't do the job; it took me nearly a decade to feel comfortable enough in myself to let that go. The turning point came one day when I entered the walk-in refrigerator to find a deep tray of food that required prep work for that evening. The tray sat on the top shelf; I could just reach it. As I began to pull it out, I realized that the tray also contained liquid, making it even heavier and more unstable. I remember briefly pausing, my good sense telling me to ask for help, a caution that I promptly disregarded ("No, I've got it"). Of course, as I pulled out the tray the liquid sloshed to the front, capsizing the tray and its contents. As I cleaned up the huge mess I had made, I realized how silly and unnecessary were my solo ways. Once I began to ask for help, I saw how it allowed me to bond with my fellow workers, and the positive effect it had on my ability, especially as a chef, to delegate authority. Improving my communication skills and bolstering my confidence didn't happen overnight, but persisted as a work in progress throughout my career.

A second significant consequence of striving to succeed in a male-dominated industry involved the suppression of my gender identity. In attempting to do a job as well as a man, I developed a tendency to perform the job like a man. It took me a long time to realize that I could use my feminine qualities and strengths to excel in my own way. Had I possessed the same self-assurance in my ability to direct a kitchen staff as I had in my talent with food and organization, I would have been a better chef. As a woman, directing men in a patriarchal society can be monumentally challenging, especially when coupled with trying to prove one's self at the same time. Rarely during my career did I find men amenable to take direction from a female chef, although exceptions to this general rule did occur. For instance, on the evening before I became the chef at a thriving restaurant in East Hampton, N.Y., I sat at their bar mid-way through the dinner rush just to observe. I wanted to see the appearance of the dinner plates as they were served, and also understand how the front of the house operated. After the kitchen slowed down, the sous chef (the position just below the chef) sat next to me to have his after-shift drink. "Florida Pete" was actually the interim chef, but he didn't want the permanent position. "So you're going to be the new chef," he began; "never saw a woman worth a damn in a restaurant kitchen." What should I have said to that? "Is that so," I muttered, but inside I'm thinking, "Oh, great, I'll just add his contempt to the stress of starting an important new job, cold, during a busy weekend." At times like this, when my fears were most acute, I would harden my resolve, refuse the option of failure, and force myself to succeed. In this case, it helped that Pete required little direction, for he knew the job and what to do before I even had to ask. Pete did test me my first day on the job by "suggesting" I make a sauce that did justice to the scrumptious roast leg of lamb special he had prepared. After I passed his test, Pete and I went on to become fast friends, respecting each other's abilities. Although I've worked with many talented people over the years, to this day I have never worked with anyone, male or female, who was such a good partner on the hot cooking line.

Unfortunately, I didn't always enjoy such good luck and over the years I suffered my share of failures and reverses. At times single parenthood, coupled with financial stress and an intense, time-consuming career, led me to utter exhaustion. In that condition, I proved unable to function well or make good life decisions. I've now worked in food service for over forty years, opening, cooking for, and managing a variety of restaurant kitchens in New York, Florida, Chicago, Maine, and California, co-owning and operating a regional Italian dinner house, and serving as a personal chef. As much as I've loved it, I've found professional cooking extremely demanding. I don't recommend the vocation to anyone unless they have a real passion for the work, which requires both physical stamina and a somewhat masochistic desire to thrive in high-stress environments.

After my husband and I retired from our respective careers in 2003 (Geoff from education), we purchased a farm in Ferndale, a small town in lush and lovely northern coastal California, just south of Eureka/Arcata. There we thrived, learning to become small-acreage farmers (raising tree and cane fruits, as well as vegetables), exceedingly grateful to have a supplemental income to help pay for our on-the-job agricultural training. We also began a small organic food manufacturing business, producing honey-sweetened preserves, natural sweetener blends, and salad dressings. We embarked on this venture working out of a commercial kitchen at our local fairgrounds. Again, we were pleased to enjoy an additional "retirement" income that helped pay for the farm's upkeep.

One of my favorite past-times while living in dairy country was watching the heifers in the pastures graze and ruminate. What fantastic role models! I rarely felt the need to formally meditate when I could look out my window or over my fence and watch this process. It automatically slowed me down, provided temporary relief from the stresses of daily life, and invited me to appreciate my connection to other living beings. Watching cattle graze—either outside my window, or in my mind's eye—grounds me and inspires gratitude. What images and scenes create such feelings in you? How might holding those visions for half a minute or so before eating help to create an atmosphere more conducive to relaxed dining and healthy digestion?

Valuing mealtime in this manner describes another way to take a small vacation from the pressures of life; it represents a true gift that we can give ourselves no matter where we live. I spend a lot of time cooking and eating, two of my greatest pleasures in life. I take small bites and chew slowly, not so much because those acts aid in the digestive process, but so I can extend my time eating. Because I enjoy it so much, I have learned to choose foods I can consume in abundance without doing myself harm. I also keep myself active, partly so that I can eat more. I love most foods – animals, grains, fruits and vegetables – but the bulk of my diet consists of vegetables, followed by whole grains, eggs, fruit, dairy, poultry, fish, and ruminants – in that order. The recipes in this book are diverse, yet they follow the lines of my personal preferences.

I create food combinations that suit my digestive system. There exist numerous food studies that can tell us what to eat, and explain the science behind healthy food consumption and digestion. Still, I let my entire being (not just my mouth), as well as my common and moral senses, dictate what works best for me. With a spectrum of sound information confirmed by our own bodies, we can become not only our most trusted nutritional resource, but also the creators of the environments that will enhance those choices.

A "Neighborhood Café," the product of my forty-plus years as a chef, represents one such environment. The business outline I will present can help in the planning of an actual business, but it can also be used in your own home with family or within a circle of friends and neighbors. This profile epitomizes my many years of both cooking delicious, healthful, and fairly simple-to-prepare foods, and of creating warm, restful, and vibrant environments. The Neighborhood Café attempts to generate an ambiance that encourages the presence and participation of everyone who enters. In the café of my mind's eye, visitors will therefore be asked to turn off their online tools before entering.

Perhaps you're wondering why I don't write a business plan, find funding, and open the café myself, instead of writing a book encouraging others. I've started my own businesses in the past and I'm proud of those accomplishments, but at my age, I'm afraid that just contemplating such labor leaves me feeling spent. Besides, in today's world asking people to turn off their cell phones before entering your business space is undoubtedly a romantic undertaking. My Neighborhood Café is a visionary one, but yours need not be.

Writing this book, which provides practical support for the café's creation, as well as examples of recipes it might serve, contributes to my grander dream of seeing these cafés pop up all over the country, perhaps even the world, and indeed to see them student-operated in all schools. My passion for this vision has its roots in a time (I was born in 1955) when many families in this country still lived near one another. During the 1950s and early 1960s almost my entire extended family lived within three New York City boroughs, Brooklyn, the Bronx, and Queens. Large family dinners took place on Sundays, and often included close friends as well as family, for I knew and played with the children on my block and in my neighborhood on a daily basis. Most evenings throughout the spring, summer, and fall, the first kid on our block to finish dinner would go outside and whistle for all to hurry up and play, whether it be stickball, stoop ball, or hide-and-go-seek, to name a few of my favorites. Most of us didn't go back indoors until it got dark and our parents called us twice. For many years, I felt like a failure as a mother because I was unable to give this gift of neighborhood camaraderie and warmth to my son, feelings that I had been so fortunate to experience as I grew up. It seems as if our culture lost a great deal when increasing geographical mobility scattered families and friends across the continent. I know I did.

My search for a sense of community, and my passion for wholesome food, has brought me here. Whether or not you someday feel compelled to open or patronize a Neighborhood Café, I hope that you enjoy this book, and come away with a positive response to the values and possibilities it represents.

CHAPTER 2

A Neighborhood Café

My book creates a standard for an indoor/outdoor café that serves high-quality coffees and teas, as well as delicious, healthful, whole food savories and sweets. The café will also serve as an information center that encourages civic engagement in both the local community and beyond. These two aspects of the café - its emphasis on food and community - go hand in hand. Most people are not likely to enjoy the full health benefits of eating well in a stressful environment; at the same time, they are unlikely to enjoy the full health benefits of a restful or vibrant environment while eating unhealthy food.

Hopefully, the good food and beverages served, and the diversity of literature found there, will attract people to the café. The Information Center will play a major role in contributing to the type of atmosphere I'm looking to create, one of encouraging people to connect to what is unperturbed and positive in us, and of providing the information that will support those connections outside the café's doors. The aromas, flavors, and information will be there for anyone wanting a break from the negativity that too often pervades our culture. The café embodies a space where people will be off-line and unavailable for the duration of their visit; it acts as a place to relax and rejuvenate. . .or not. You may only want to come in for a cup of coffee or a snack to go (bring your reusable containers!)

and leave as quickly as you can. My vision of the café focuses simply on calling attention to some of the helpful and practical ideas being tested by people in their communities around the world.

There's certainly no shortage in the news of friction and cruelty amongst people everywhere, making it at times too easy to imagine the worst about our world. Yet most people, in all countries, want peace, freedom, and a fair way to support themselves and their families. We all possess the capacity to love, to learn, and to be kind; we also can hate, reject, and be mean-spirited. Our individual leanings come primarily from what we're shown and taught to believe as we grow, and the way we interpret those teachings according to our immediate environment and past experiences. The more we accept and respect people as the interaction between their personal experiences and their surrounding cultures, the sooner we'll be able to replace fear and blame with empathy and inclusiveness. Our so-called individuality is very much conditional, not nearly all we are and all we can be.

Ferndale, where I lived for eleven years, including the five most precious ones with my husband before his death, is a town both conservative and liberal. For the sake of peaceful co-existence, Geoff and I decided early on (after we hosted a disastrous dinner party) to avoid talk of religion and politics, and we were rewarded by a genuine intimacy with many of our neighbors who we might otherwise not have known. I was honored to meet people on a level beyond their political views and religious convictions (and to have them meet me in that spirit as well). Going beneath the surface of contingent matters to who we are in our hearts remains a lesson in open-mindedness that I'll forever cherish.

All religions preach core values of love, kindness, and generosity, qualities that people, religious or not, fundamentally share. When we look beyond our fortified selves, we see how deeply similar we all are, and from that more humble position we can create an environment where extremism, from any direction, won't thrive. The responsibility to get along with each other is ours. Nothing substantial and lasting will happen until we learn it for ourselves first. This makes it all the more important to act in accordance (as much as we can) with the vision we individually choose to hold for our collective futures – not someone else's vision and certainly not the accepted "continued greedy and violent future" many see as inevitable. Hopefully, most of us possess the capability to govern our thoughts and actions, replacing outraged, impatient, discouraged, anxious thoughts with their opposite forms. Whenever we open our hearts and look not to control or judge, but to help and accept others, we create the type of community upon which this book depends.

With a focus on a clean and healthful food supply, I intend to show that tentative solutions to our shared dilemmas already exist, rehearsed in small communities and large by individuals and groups around the globe. The Neighborhood Café will be a place to foster inspiration and problem-solving, where one can see the best in people, including ourselves, and find many delicious and wholesome things to eat and drink. The environment will be a comfortable one, perhaps adorned with a rotation of attractive art produced by community artists, and background music (which can be local as well) that is neither jarring nor "spacey," to further cultivate the creative climate.

In the coming chapters, I will highlight both the larger issues raised by the types of literature I imagine being part of a neighborhood café's information center, and the more mundane nuts and bolts of putting together a professionally run small food business. I will address the structures of employee-owned and cooperatively run businesses, including a consideration of pricing and costs, and discuss as well some of the more humble culinary traditions that contributed to my vision of a neighborhood café, including ideas and recipes for new school bake sales and old school lemonade stands.

Although I'll be providing a food professional's overview of a business model for a neighborhood café, I've already suggested that the café needn't be a business at all. It can be as simple as weekly get-togethers with friends and neighbors for a healthy meal or snack, and conversation that might culminate in a simple community action like a phone call, a letter, an email, or perhaps a visit to the office of your local representative. It can become a habitual family activity during meal times (or long car rides) when thinking about, and listing, possible solutions to particular problems can become a regular part of one's day. Even those living alone can join in this activity. The most important aspect of the "Neighborhood Café" is the intent to bring focused, constructive ideas and healthy foods to the community table, even when it's a table for one. Those objectives can be met almost anywhere, by anyone, at little or no additional cost, and with as much time as is available.

Conceiving of the human as separate from the rest of the planet and from each other dooms us to the unsatisfying realm of our frustrations and conceit, to a materialist, anxiety-ridden, and convenience-based culture that makes healthy change almost impossible. The Neighborhood Café, on the other hand, imagines a world in which all living creatures share a past, present, and collective future. It asks us to develop new habits of thought and behavior that allow us to thrive, and that sanction the power of the collective human spirit over the narrow concerns of ego and self.

CHAPTER 3

The Information Center

I have designed the Neighborhood Café to promote self- and civic-empowerment and inspire its owners, staff, and customers. Its existence will depend upon nourishing bodies with good food, nourishing intellects with uplifting knowledge and unifying engagement, and, as a business, affording staff and owners a livable income. It will honor the process over the end and put its customers at ease so that they can choose how much they wish to participate, if at all. Central to this mission is my vision of the Information Center. There are other methods, some similar, that groups use to work through challenges and facilitate solutions. This is but one approach.

As customers await their orders, they're invited to browse through the Information Center for something of interest to take to their table and read. The center simply consists of three long rectangular tables preferably positioned in a way that provides access for people to walk along both long sides of each table.

One table will provide information about local, national, and global organizations that are facilitating solutions for many of today's most pressing challenges. Since the Neighborhood Café will encourage peaceful co-existence, it will avoid contentious concerns that may only lead to division and conflict. Many issues interest most people no matter their political and religious affiliations:

malnutrition and obesity, physical abuse, human trafficking, lack of access to well-paying employment or to affordable quality education for our nation's children are examples of topics that might not raise partisan hostility. As we look at creative approaches to such issues perhaps we can begin to offer and support exploratory and proven solutions to the seemingly insoluble problems that confront us. This table will identify some of the many innovative organizations exploring such problems, and the information offered will look to the resourceful responses already being put in place, and not the problems themselves.

Another table provides information about national and global organizations that can serve as alternatives to the Armed Forces. Young people enlist in the military for many reasons beyond the conviction that serving their country represents the right thing to do. Some feel the need to belong to a community, to receive an education and training, to enjoy a structured environment in which to learn discipline and how to become an adult; others may want to travel to exotic places, to earn an early pension, to flee from poverty or an abusive or dysfunctional home. However, there exist peaceful ways to serve our country that offer many of these benefits, and that may provide perhaps better outcomes for the individual and the planet. A strong peace-building force can strengthen our friendly ties and alliances around the world, which in turn would benefit our military. Our Armed Forces would be well served by supporting already existing non-military programs with increased benefits and visibility on school campuses, especially where they already recruit. The more options our young people have, the more useful and fulfilling their lives can become. This table will be dedicated to those options, some of which include opportunities for people of different age groups, including seniors.

The last of the three tables houses the Forum. The Forum provides the play area for interaction between customers, and the birthing of new, or the resurrecting of old ideas. Most ideas will simply disappear into oblivion if they cannot begin to assume a concrete form. One of my career goals as a young woman, for instance, was to start my own restaurant, regardless of the fact that until I turned forty I lived paycheck-to-paycheck as a single working mother. It wasn't until

I described my restaurant on paper in the form of a business plan (so detailed that I had the sensation of actually operating it) that opportunities arose to help me realize my dream. This table in the café will be the place where "blueprints" are born, where fleeting and insubstantial ideas begin to take tangible form. The following description suggests how I see the Forum operating.

One specific question, directed to a particular dilemma or social issue, will be asked every third or fourth month. I specify three to four months because I think it would encourage more carefully wrought strategies for long-term solutions rather than quick fixes that commonly ignore their often unintended consequences. As well, that time frame is likely to be more practical for a majority of people who don't have large blocks of time to spend on the process. An example of a question might be, "What organization can we design, or partner with, that would offer all children and teens in our community engaging and enriching places to go when not in school, and assure that they arrive there and home safely?"

After the Neighborhood Café poses a question, customers will be asked to disregard financial concerns and practicality, and to address only their highest ideal for a solution, which can be presented anonymously or not. These dated responses will go directly into a slot on a rack (like a revolving postcard display) for customers to read throughout the first three to four weeks; they will be invited to highlight with a check-mark the ideas they like the best. In the spirit of the Neighborhood Café, they will be asked only to check the ideas they like, and not to respond to ideas they don't like. At the end of this stage, staff will take one to two weeks, depending on the size of the response, to identify and print out the most popular ideas. Copies of the results will be made using recycled paper and presented on the forum table.

At this point, issues of practicality and money can be addressed. For the next month, customers can choose ideas from the master list and elaborate on the original proposal. They might also use ideas offered by some of the organizations listed on one of the forum tables. They will date their additions (so customers can more easily identify the newer responses) and place their input on the revolving stands for others to see. Should anyone want to contribute to a particular item with time, money, connections, or a simple action, they would add that information, along with their name and contact information, or communicate their intent to a staff member.

Although connecting individuals with specific non-profits may be one possible outcome of the Forum, the Neighborhood Café is not in the fundraising or recruiting business. Its primary mission is to nourish, inform, and inspire its community. The café will reflect the common belief that our evolution starts as an inward journey that then extends out to affect others. That journey commonly describes a never-ending path concerned with developing strength of character; it is not directed towards material objects or seeking answers from outside the individual. I intend the Neighborhood Café to operate at the forefront of a directed, positive, expanding human growth movement which, while recognizing our capacity to act selfishly, heedlessly, and combatively, insists that individual choice can lead us to healthier and more positive modes of behavior.

Near the end of the second month, as the Forum process proceeds, and customers continue to offer more detailed suggestions, the staff will take three to four weeks to draft a blueprint based on the information they receive. If they require more input, they will pass along their requests in writing; otherwise, they will present the blueprint via the Forum table. The final stage of the process will introduce the initial steps needed to carry the model forward, whatever positive form it takes, and the small or large impact it might make on the particular problem addressed. Among other actions, some might include sending copies of the blueprint to local organizations, local media, and even to our local, state, or federal representatives; when necessary and feasible, further action may be required. The entire procedure will then repeat itself with a new question to answer, a new issue to address. The Neighborhood Café will put out an annual summary depicting the progress of any projects that result through its efforts.

It is both my hope and belief that after a time of working collectively to respond to questions that don't lead to division and defensiveness, we will naturally hone our abilities to cooperate, and become better able to address all complex issues as a community.

POTENTIAL QUESTIONS FOR THE NEIGHBORHOOD CAFÉ

Many types of questions can be asked at the café. Sometimes they will delve into local, sometimes state, or even federal issues, although many questions will involve all three levels of government. Occasionally, the questions will focus on the individual, as in, "What specific actions or responses can change a non-beneficial habit or behavior?" A question on a mixed state and local level might be, "What program can we develop or partner with that will train local workers, and help with job placement for those affected by declining industries and opportunities?" An ensuing question may directly tie into a previous question, as in this case: "What environmentally sound infrastructure project can we create on a local level that will generate jobs?"

Also on a local level, we might ask, "How may we successfully teach our children and teenagers non-violent communication, self-respect, and respect for others despite the fact that disrespect characterizes today's media and politics?"

Such big questions might alternate with simpler ones. Indeed, at first less complex inquiries might work better, questions like the following eliciting a variety of precise answers: "What improvements can we make to our local playgrounds so they can be enjoyed by children with disabilities?" "What are specific ways we can beautify our neighborhood?"

Research will normally be necessary to address most issues and problems. The Neighborhood Café can offer background information that might help define the questions they pose but should be careful about providing such information, lest it overly influences the individual customers whose responses should come from their own hearts and minds, as well as their own research. Research can often lead us in unexpected directions. For example, when I was looking into issues concerning sustainable agriculture, I came across references to "victory gardens," a subject I knew little about. As defined on Wikipedia, "Victory gardens …. were vegetable, fruit, and herb gardens planted at private residences and public parks in the United States, United Kingdom, Canada, Australia and Germany during World War I and World War II." Sarah Sundin, writing about WW2, notes that just a few years after the U.S. federal government re-established a Victory Garden program in 1941, some 20 million gardens were planted. By 1943, "these little plots produced 40 percent of all vegetables consumed in the US. It's estimated that 9-10 million tons of vegetables were grown….Neighborhood and community committees were formed with veteran gardeners guiding newcomers. These committees also helped with distribution of surplus food and sharing of equipment. Victory Gardens were promoted as family fun, as good healthy recreation for all ages. They sprang up on farms, in backyards, and on city rooftops." Many businesses planted gardens on their properties for use in company cafeterias, and schoolyard gardens provided fresh vegetables for school lunches. Popular periodicals published articles about preserving food for the winter months and encouraged sharing surplus production within the neighborhood.

The Neighborhood Café could present this basic research, and then ask the question, "Working with local government and/or non-profits…how can we successfully resurrect and encourage the establishment of 'Victory Gardens' within our community as was done extensively throughout the U.S. during WWII?"

It's easy to get overloaded with too much information at one time, even good information. For this reason, The Neighborhood Café will limit highlighted organizations at the Information Center to perhaps six or seven in each of four or five categories. Every third month or so, many of those listings will be rotated out (sometimes just temporarily) to showcase other groups and, sometimes, other topics. Information about each organization will be primarily confined to their mission, with brief examples of current projects and past successes. Contact information will be included for anyone wishing to know more about a particular group.

The Information Center will also include a revolving rack specifically set aside for inspirational articles that might include references to other organizations. Besides tales of successful projects, an inspirational article might also open peoples' hearts and minds to a new way of looking at a subject. One example of that can be found on the welcomehomesoldier.com website, written by veteran Edward Tick. I recommend this important inspiring article to all, not just to veterans. As well, the rack might hold a referral to an article on a website that contains encouraging and practical information. As an example, the "41 Most Innovative K-12 Schools in America" on noodle.com, might be highlighted as a helpful tool when the current question being asked at the café pertains to education.

What follows are examples of categories and organizations that you might find on the tables at a Neighborhood Café's Information Center:

CLEANING OUR FOOD SUPPLY

1. OFRF – Organic Farming Research Foundation
2. The Savory Institute
3. Humane Farming Association
4. IFOAM – Organics International and IFOAM North America
5. NSAC – National Sustainable Agriculture Coalition
6. Food First
7. Organic Seed Alliance

EDUCATION

1. Diploma Plus
2. Room to Read
3. College Summit – Peer Forward
4. Ashoka
5. Khan Academy and Khan Academy Kids
6. OIC of America
7. Citizen Schools

ALTERNATIVES TO THE MILITARY

1. AmeriCorps programs, including DSU - Disaster Service Unit, National Civilian Community Corps, Vista, National Conservation Corps, Student Conservation Corps, City Years Corps, and Senior Corps
2. SCA - Student Conservation Association
3. Peaceful Career Alternatives – peacefulcareers.org
4. Nonviolent Peace Force
5. Peace Corps
6. WWOOF - Worldwide Organization of Organic Farmers

ACCESS TO HEALTHY FOOD

1. FoodCorps
2. Wholesome Wave
3. National Farm to School Network
4. Voices for Healthy Kids
5. Healthy Food Access Portal
6. The Food Trust – The National Healthy Corner Store Network
7. HFFI – Healthy Food Financing Initiative

The following is an example of what one full listing might look like:

FoodCorps: Their website, foodcorps.org, defines their mission as, "Together with communities, FoodCorps serves to connect kids to healthy food in school."

Current Projects
• Working with educators to teach gardening, cooking, and tasting in classrooms across the nation; research suggests that children love foods they've grown and prepared themselves.

- Sprout Scouts is a skills-based program developed by FoodCorps and *Life Lab* that provides FoodCorps service members the resources and activities they need to teach their students about cooking, gardening, and nutrition through hands-on learning. Similar to the Boy and Girl Scouts, Sprout Scouts proceeds through a series of adventures that develop new and complementary skills; it works with after-school programs as well.
- Developing nutritional protocols that can guide schools from kindergarten through high school, they hope to inspire cultural shifts and policy changes that will benefit all of our nation's schools and the health of our children.

Past Successes
- They've created numerous farm-to-school programs, collaborated with schools to develop educational gardens, improved school food, and helped incorporate nutritional education into the regular school day.
- Through their partnership with the Tisch Food Center at Teachers College, Columbia University, they determined that more than 75% of FoodCorps schools had measurably healthier nutritional environments by the end of the school year. Schools that promote FoodCorps' hands-on activities triple the number of fruits and vegetables consumed by their students.
- 161,818 students have been reached, 426 gardens supported, and 440 new foods introduced while encouraging school communities to celebrate healthy food.

MEDIA'S FUNCTION

It's not unrealistic to imagine a world in which people genuinely get along with each other, enjoying helpful, cooperative relationships, and finding joy by contributing to the common good. Such relationships hopefully characterize our own lives; they certainly exist all around the globe, and we need to attend more carefully to those stories, feeding that vision while tuning out the tweets, manipulated stories and videos, and toxic political talk that keep many people divided, afraid, and contemptuous of others.

Reliable data is essential to The Information Center, and finding it might be challenging at times. As difficult as it can be to sift through the one-sided stories, exaggerations, stereotypical depictions, news blurred by opinion, statistics and quotes taken out of context, and even outright falsehoods, we must try. The more we hear distortions repeated, the more we tend to regard them as truths. As consumers, we have the power to direct our media outlets to give us conscientious and accurate information, uplifting because it's constructive. That power resides in our willingness to tune in and click on the models we want to support, turn off what we don't, and the voice to explain why.

The instinctive wariness I inherited from growing up in New York City with an attentive father has prepared me well for this day and age. I didn't always listen to my dad, but I did when he told me during one of our political conversations, "Darling, you need to think for yourself because our government and big business are often in cahoots, and even when not, they don't necessarily have our best interests at heart." Although upstanding local, daily, and comprehensive investigative reporting remains vital to our democracy, media, in all its varied forms, too often represents the interests of big business. I try to always begin by questioning the origin of the information I receive, and the intent of those broadcasting it. Reporters, like all people, interpret the world, even facts, through their individual perspectives, which make it nearly impossible to find a news story void of bias. However, there exists an important distinction between those natural levels of bias and intentional misrepresentation. I pay little heed to news and opinions from any source that attempts to initiate a self-righteous, blameful, fearful, or furious reaction. We possess the awareness and intelligence to think through and articulate fair and helpful solutions to our problems, expanding the countless good works already underway rather than spending our time and energy on mere outrage and negativity.

Reading or hearing the same sensationalized news and headlines again and again might be one cause of the pervasive unease that currently characterizes our society. We now seem prisoners of a 24/7 news market that operates like a soap opera: you can watch it every Monday and automatically know everything that happened the previous week; the continuity and selective repetition (along with "new sound bites you won't want to miss!") are part of its addictive attraction. If mainstream and social media ever became a format for in-depth coverage of positive news occurring around the planet, and in our cities and states as well, I might be in danger of becoming addicted. "They" say that bad, offensive, sensationalized news sells because that's what people want, but I don't agree. The media industry fosters our addiction to that type of news because addictions increase business. We could just as easily become addicted to news that arouses inspiration, analytical thought, and caring engagement, but we're more vulnerable and easily steered when feeling angry, afraid, deficient, and/or discouraged. For now, we must instead consciously protect ourselves and our young from those "reeling in" strategies constantly put before us by the media and other industries.

Perhaps, unfortunately, there will always be a market for skewed news. Many of us gravitate towards ideas and opinions acquired from childhood and beyond that validate our own, or that make us feel part of a social group. The danger in this lies in the possibility that after a while those out-sourced ideas and opinions will become our own without our even recognizing it. I hope that one day most of us will see each other apart from our easily shaped opinions. We'll stop seeking "solutions" that only benefit "our side." We'll mature from the need to define people by their dissimilarities or blame or do harm to others to feel better about ourselves and our society. Too engaged to bother with such destructive behaviors, our immeasurable potential and constructive actions will instead empower us.

"Constructive Journalism" is an expanding global movement within journalism that informs and empowers the consumer by supplying them with more context and knowledge, giving a more balanced and realistic view of the world.

According to consructivejournalism.org, they promote "reporting that includes positive [not fluffy] and solution-focused elements...while upholding journalism's core functions and ethics." The Constructive Journalism Network website states that their model investigates and takes note of the common ground, progress, learning, resources, constructive conversation, and co-creation that their listeners and readership experience. These organizations are dedicated to creating opportunities for that form of journalism to flourish over biased, polarizing news. Solutions Journalism Network is a non-profit, independent organization that also promotes evidence-based reporting. Their storytracker.solutionsjournalism.org website contains a curated database of articles they've collected and tagged that provide the reader with "coverage of effective or promising ideas and approaches - by issue, location, journalist, and success factor." The Information Center at a Neighborhood Café will showcase this type of journalism. The more we support models like these for our news, the more quickly we will lead mainstream and social media to follow suit, insisting that they use responsibly their immense power to shape our world.

If we want to live in a better world, we're the ones who will need to initiate and shape it. When I owned my own restaurant, I never thought of hiring a manager and simply telling her or him to "Look around, and have at it." Our government, at the local, state, and federal levels, functions as our managers, and we must explain in detail what we want them to do for us. It's our business, our money, and our beautiful, diverse country. If we're not the general managers, then we're the managed. If we remain divided and pitted against each other, others will continue to manipulate us. Finding common ground remains essential to our ability to delegate. Surely we can agree on some solutions to housing and caring for our war veterans and community residents most in need, having clean air to breathe, clean water to drink, and clean food to eat, and providing training, job placement, and dignified living and working conditions for all in our community.

We can choose to put our differences aside; we can refuse to attend to the distractions that prevent us from becoming part of the solutions we want to experience. When we help create an environment where people in our neighborhood have each other's best interests at heart, we will see less crime, fewer addicts and suicides, and a reduction in self-absorption and greed, homelessness, human trafficking, incarceration, and stress. As David Brooks writes in an excellent New York Times op-ed piece on improving schools through good leadership, "We went through a period when we believed you could change institutions without first changing the character of the people in them. But we were wrong. Social transformation follows personal transformation." And although that concept is true to build any culture for lasting change, we mustn't use it as an excuse for inaction today, but rather work concurrently on personal evolution and changing systems that breed inequities and dysfunction. Those efforts are intrinsically tied together and fuel each other. Enthusiasm usually follows success, which is why new behaviors can be so difficult to adopt; but once we take the first steps and begin to experience minor successes, enthusiasm will grow and spread.

Without envisioning solutions clearly, we can't create and bring them to fruition. The Information Center offers one approach to developing and clarifying answers to some of the most important issues we face today. I'm sure that adjustments will be necessary to fine-tune the process. I see the Information Center as a "manual" system, but I have no doubt that it can also be translated into a digital format, just not by me. I'm an archaic specimen in this modern era; I know little more than the basics of the digital world that I have yet to embrace. By choice, I have no experience with social media. Still, I can see social media as a valuable tool in its potential to create a platform for a Neighborhood Café. Again, I won't be the one to figure that out. For whoever might, I can only hope that the intent to keep it a positive, inclusive, and conciliatory arena will be fundamental to its creation and evolution.

CHAPTER 4

On Cooking and Eating; Recipes for A Neighborhood Café

Cooking and baking are learned arts and most people who enjoy them can become proficient. Fundamental to this enjoyment, oddly enough, is the refusal to become attached to the results of your efforts. Everyone—particularly professionals—suffer disappointments in the kitchen. We don't, of course, strive for failure, but if you can't summon your creativity, modify recipes on the fly and court possible failure, you will never learn to fully enjoy and experience the artistic nature behind the culinary process.

Creating recipes for this book represented a significant personal challenge because I'm naturally a "little of this, little of that" type of cook. Having to pin myself down and measure every ingredient, and disrupt my rhythm to measure again when an adjustment was needed, proved difficult indeed, often requiring many attempts to work through the same recipe. This process of revision, in fact, calls into question the very idea of "creating recipes," because all recipes possess an extended history that predates their apparently final articulation in this or any book. The recipes in this book already existed in some form prior to my development of them. I've revised and tweaked them enough to make them "my own," but where they may have originated, or who introduced me to them, for the most part, I can no longer remember. Even the formulas I believe that I've "invented" almost certainly existed in a similar arrangement before I constructed them. I hope that the recipes in this book will spur your imagination and be re-created by you as they take on new revisions along their evolutionary route. Indeed, this process of reinvention might structure an interesting movie, the running history of a single recipe throughout the centuries, a food version of "The Red Violin."

∾

I don't begin each baked goods recipe with preheating instructions, but rather leave it to the baker to turn the oven to the instructed temperature when appropriate to do so, usually 10–18 minutes before needed. For cookies, quick breads, and cakes, after transferring the batter into the prepared sheet, loaf or cake pan, I recommend that you push the batter gently from the center towards the sides of the pan with a spoon. This will help create a slight rise in the center, but not so much that the bottom or ends will over-bake before the center cooks through. Unless you have a convection oven or are lucky enough to have a superior oven that heats the front, back, and sides evenly, turn your baked goods around once in the oven halfway through their projected cooking time; check if done, approximately 5 minutes before the recommended timing, or sooner if what you're baking seems to be cooking quickly.

Stored flours settle, and sifting them when preparing your batter will bring them back from their compacted state. You needn't have a special tool to sift your dry ingredients for that purpose. Simply stir the flour with a spoon before measuring, lifting flour and spoon from the bottom up; this will loosen the grains and enable you to measure the flour more accurately. Do the same with baking powder, baking soda and cocoa powder and break up any clumps with the back of a spoon. If you want to lightly boost the nutritional content of a baked goods batter, substitute 1/4 – 1/3 cup of oat bran for that amount of flour. You can also add 1/4 cup of sesame seeds, chopped unsalted pumpkin seeds, sunflower seeds, or nuts to the dry ingredient mix if that sounds appealing and the batter doesn't already call for nuts or seeds.

If a recipe calls for buttermilk and you have none on hand, whisk plain yogurt with milk or water to buttermilk consistency. Start with a 3-1 ratio and add more liquid if needed. You can also stir together 1 Tbsp. of freshly squeezed lemon juice or distilled white vinegar per cup of milk; let the mixture sit for 10 minutes to allow it to thicken a bit. If your baked good recipe calls for a liquid sweetener, lightly grease the measuring tool with oil first. The sweetener will slide off easily into the bowl.

⁓

Having your ingredients prepped in advance is key to efficient cooking and generally yields the best results with the least stress. If the ingredients list of a recipe in this book doesn't specify the size of a fruit or vegetable, choose a medium-sized product, except for eggs, which should be large. Maple syrup should always be pure. I developed all these recipes using unsalted butter, nuts, and seeds, as well as pure vanilla extract, one or two percent milk, dried leaf thyme, extra virgin olive oil, mineral sea salt, and freshly ground pepper; I highly recommend their use.

When I cook with wine, I use decent table wines and fortified wines, like dry sherry, dry Marsala, and Madeira; I use dry vermouth in place of white wine for its pleasing herbal quality. The addition of ingredients like wine, butter, oil, cream, rich broths, and more varied spices, when used moderately, will enhance many dishes. However, most of the recipes in this book are designed to be flavorful, but also utilitarian, requiring less expansive pantries and meant for everyday consumption.

The recipes in this chapter, and in chapter six, are representative of wholesome baked goods that would go well in a café setting, especially one asking for their customer's simultaneous engagement in other activities. For the same reasons, these foods work well in office settings and at other communal gatherings, including bake sales and fundraisers. The recipes in chapters seven and eight are designed for people who want to make changes to their diets for health, financial, or ethical reasons, and for those who want to build upon their repertoire of enjoyable dishes. Developing new practices are critical to a healthy evolution on earth and the quality of the foods we consume daily is an essential part of that progression. The recipes in this book reflect my professional experience, my personal taste and ideals, and my desire to nourish the body. However, I am not a nutritionist or medical professional of any kind. The nutritional information I've written throughout this book has come from careful research and my interpretation of that research as a layperson. If you have a compromised medical condition, please consult your doctor before making changes to your diet.

ᕙᕗ

I don't specify organic ingredients in my recipes, but I encourage their use as much as possible, especially for the foods most likely to retain the most pesticide (including glyphosate) residues, referenced in Chapter Seven.

Because many nutrients reside just under the skin of fresh vegetables, I rarely peel anything, unless it has been waxed. I make exceptions for winter squash, rutabaga, and other tough-skinned tubers, but I never peel potatoes. I simply scrub and rinse most fruits and vegetables with clean water before preparing them.

When cooking with dried herbs, use too few rather than too many, for they can easily overpower the taste of a dish or impart an off-putting flavor. If I had to choose five essential ingredients for my kitchen, they would be extra virgin olive oil, lemon, garlic, sea salt, and pepper. Good cooking often depends on simplicity: most savory dishes will taste delicious with just these five ingredients. Yet I would sorely miss Indian, Moroccan, Asian, and the many other cuisines that depend on their unique and delicious blend of spices and other flavorings.

When I call for grated pasta cheese I often specify Romano (Pecorino Romano), because I particularly enjoy the flavor and texture of the sheep's milk used to produce it. You can of course substitute Parmesan or Asiago, also delicious cheeses that work just as well as Romano; the former has the advantage of being more readily available. However, I encourage you to purchase blocks or wedges, if you can, and grate them fresh as needed.

In my kitchen, I use low-fat milk, yogurt, and sour cream that contain no added chemicals. To me, a non-fat product ceases to be a whole food, while a full-fat product often contains more fat calories than I like to consume. In that same vein, when I fix myself an egg dish using 2 eggs, I'll sometimes leave out half a yolk and save myself 25 calories of fat. This represents a good trade-off for me. I like to extend my daily fat intake throughout the day, leaving enough to consume with dinner, my favorite meal. I'm not advocating for being thin and I'm not an athlete looking for optimal fitness. My objective is to balance what I emotionally want to eat or drink with what my body will thrive on and I attempt to encourage that point of view throughout this book knowing it will mean something different for everyone. All body types require a daily intake of fat. It's not simply a matter of the number of calories our bodies can use and store healthfully; the quality of the fat we consume is equally important. "Good fats" include what is present in nuts and seeds, avocados, olives (and the oils extracted from those foods), and fatty fish, like salmon, trout, oysters, sardines, anchovies, and herring. I don't keep jarred mayonnaise in my kitchen, but rather use olive oil and vinegar, or mashed avocado, sometimes along with a bit of plain yogurt and/or Dijon mustard, to spread on bread for sandwiches, and to prepare tuna, chicken, and egg salads. In general, I hold to a moderate daily consumption of unsaturated fats as much as I can.

Most commercial salad dressings are high in fat. The next time you finish a bottle of store-bought dressing, instead of tossing the bottle, wash it and fill with 1/4 cup each of balsamic and red wine vinegar, and 1/2 cup of water. Add 1-1/4 tsp. of salt, 1 Tbsp. of maple syrup or lightly warmed (if necessary for blending) honey, and 1/4 cup plus 1 Tbsp. of olive oil. Shake vigorously before each use to keep the oil evenly distributed; do not store it in the refrigerator unless for an extended period and allow the dressing to come to room temperature before using. As options for the basic recipe, add any of the following: 1 or 2 cloves of finely minced or pressed garlic, 1 Tbsp. of Dijon mustard (to prevent lumps, dilute Dijon to a pourable state with a small amount of the dressing before adding to the bottle), 2 Tbsp. of finely grated Romano cheese, 2 Tbsp. of finely chopped parsley.

I enjoy eating meat and fish that remain attached to the bone, for the bone adds flavor and moisture to the finished dish. As a peasant eater, I enjoy getting my fingers dirty and taking the extra time necessary to gnaw the meat closest to the bone. When my son Danny and I had our dog, Nute, I imagined that she rolled her eyes at me whenever I handed her one of my picked-clean bones.

When I call for skin-on chicken parts and my recipe fails to produce crispy skin, remove the skin just before serving. Before cooking, trim the chicken parts of all excess fat and skin (and disinfect your cutting board afterward). If you're fortunate enough to have the services of a butcher available to you, have him, or her, thoroughly trim the pieces for you. Preparing chicken with some of its skin allows the meat to retain more of its moisture through the cooking process; at the same time, the fat remaining after trimming renders and flavors the sauce. If the skin cooks up especially crispy, I can't resist it; I leave it on and serve it intact.

I prepare vegetables and pasta al dente – cooked, but still firm. Vegetables lose nutrients the longer they cook; besides yielding a lovely texture, pasta cooked al dente provides the body with steady sustained energy, but, when cooked past al dente, it releases more sugars and increases blood sugar levels. Pasta, vegetables, and meats, while still very hot, continue to cook after they're removed from the heat, so determine, through practice, what minor adjustments you may want to make so that your meals end up cooked to your satisfaction.

≈

If you intend to open a Neighborhood Café (or even if you don't), you might want to give some thought to the types of cookware you use. Roughly 70% of all skillets sold in the U.S. last year had non-stick surfaces. According to many experts in the fields of science and health, the chemicals used to manufacture these non-stick coatings raise significant health concerns. Among the dozens of conflicting reports and major studies on the subject, the Good Housekeeping Institute conducted its own testing, including interviews with experts. Their findings, published on the Good Housekeeping website, concluded that over-heating represents the major concern when cooking in a non-stick pan. When the pans get too hot, "the coating may begin to break down at the molecular level, and toxic particles and gases, some of them carcinogenic, can be released." The article lists ways to use non-stick cookware safely: "Any food that cooks quickly on low or medium heat and coats most of the pan's surface (which brings down the pan's temperature) is unlikely to cause problems." They recommend that you never preheat an empty pan, sear meats, or cook anything over high heat, or for a prolonged period (these heat limitations make them impractical for many restaurant applications). They also recommend keeping your kitchen ventilated while cooking in such pans, not using metal utensils, or steel wool and other abrasives when cleaning the pans, and, if you store them stacked, separating them with paper towels to avoid scratches. Choose a heavier non-stick pan over a lighter-weight one when purchasing and replacing this cookware every few years: "if pans do chip or flake, they may be more likely to release toxic compounds," says Kannan of the New York State Dept. of Health. If your non-stick cookware becomes damaged, chipped, or is flaking off, he says "throw it out."

Most professional kitchens I've worked in utilize stainless steel, carbon steel, cast iron, and aluminum pots and pans (although aluminum can react poorly when used to cook acidic foods). These are typically found in new and used wholesale restaurant supply stores. Many of these stores are open to the public and are precisely where one would likely go to furnish a Neighborhood Café. In my home kitchen, I don't use coated non-stick cookware. Most of my pots and pans are decades old and remain in excellent condition, largely because I season my pans to produce a non-stick surface. When I buy a new pan not already pre-seasoned, I wash it well with a non-abrasive scrubber and hot soapy water to remove any protective or packaging residue. I dry the pan thoroughly and proceed as follows for all pans I wish to season or re-season, primarily my skillets, wok, and cast-iron pans. While preheating my oven, I place the pan on a burner over low heat and add a thin layer of high-heat cooking oil that just coats the bottom, tipping the pan a bit to allow oil to run partially up the sides. Before the pan gets too hot, I wipe out the excess oil with a non-lint kitchen rag, making sure that the inner sides are completely coated. With kitchen ventilation on (and left on until the oven is turned off), I set the burner to medium-high and heat the pan until the oil begins to smoke; I remove the pan from the hot surface to another burner until cool and rub in another thin layer of oil using the same rag, making sure there are no streaks of oil remaining. For stainless steel or for a pan that doesn't have an oven-safe handle, I'll repeat the stovetop procedure at least two more times, ending with a thorough wiping out of oil residue. If the handle is oven-safe, I place the pan in a 375-degree oven for 50 minutes, for cast iron or carbon steel, and 20 minutes for aluminum or tin. Without opening the oven door, I let the pan cool in the oven, remove and wipe it clean of excess oil; the pan is now ready to use or be stored (between a non-lint cloth or paper towel if stacked). It's important to wipe the pan well before storing it to avoid getting a build-up of oil that will turn tacky if allowed to develop. You want your pan to have a smooth, blotch-free surface. Certain metals will darken during the seasoning process as well as through use and oxidation. This "patina" will develop into a nice protective coating for your pan.

I enjoy making omelettes and "over-easy" eggs and have a favorite pan designated just for that purpose. I use a wooden spoon to cook with and no soap or water to clean my egg pan; instead, I simply wipe it with a lightly oiled cloth while still warm. When cooking in my other seasoned skillets, I use primarily wooden utensils to avoid scratching the pan's surface. If the pan needs soaking after use, I do so after the pan has cooled. Exposing an empty hot pan to water that's cooler than the pan's surface can warp its bottom. To clean, I use mild soap when needed, warm water, and a gentle pad or sponge. I dry the pan, warm it over low heat on the stovetop, and thoroughly rub in a small amount of oil. When cool, I hang it or store it stacked between a non-lint cloth.

Basically, the non-stick layer you will have created for your pans is baked-on oil, and you want to preserve that layer as well as you can. Caring for your cookware in these ways can be quite satisfying; once you make a habit of it, the process takes hardly any time at all.

Because I emphasize easy and quick preparations for the majority of recipes in this book, I call for canned beans instead of dried, although cooked dried beans are always better than canned. If you have the time, by all means, cook beans from scratch. I've included a general recipe for cooking beans listed in the index at the end of this book. For a similar reason, I call for crushed red chile flakes and red Tabasco sauce (or use another brand that contains only hot peppers, vinegar, and salt) in the place of fresh hot chiles; there are occasions when I don't want to take the extra time to handle fresh hot peppers and the thorough clean-up they require, but if you have no problem using them, again, by all means, substitute the fresh for the dried or liquid, to your taste. As well, if you have fresh English peas, corn, or leafy greens available to you, use them in place of their frozen form.

Although I don't specify it in the many recipes that include garlic, it is always peeled. A quick way to peel garlic is to smash the cloves by carefully banging (or pressing down on) each one with the flat side of your knife blade (meat mallet or pestle) until the clove is slightly crushed. The skin will fall off easily.

When I dine out, I always appreciate it when I'm given an ample serving of vegetables with the meals I order. I am not a vegetarian, but I love my vegetables, and at home, I strive to incorporate more of them into my meals without dirtying an extra pan. When I heat soup for lunch, for example, I throw a big handful of baby greens, or torn spinach and lettuce, into the bowl and pour the hot soup over them. While cooking pasta, I add to the colander thinly shredded cabbage, kale, chard, spinach, escarole, broccoli rabe, or/and whole frozen peas. When the pasta is done, I pour the boiling salted pasta water over them to lightly cook, and toss the vegetables together with the pasta and sauce, or plate them on the side sprinkled with a little lemon. I often line part of my dinner plate with fresh baby greens, spinach, or arugula and top them with my hot entrée to lightly wilt. I keep zucchini, yellow squash, snow or snap peas on hand not only because I like them, but because they cook quickly. If I find extra room in the pan in which I'm cooking dinner, I'll throw them in during the last 2–3 minutes. If there's no extra room, I plate my meal and, as soon as I've emptied the pan, I add the peas, chopped leafy greens, or thinly sliced summer squash, a pinch of salt (and lemon juice if using greens), and a little water to mix with the delicious bits in the bottom of the pan. I steam the vegetables, covered, for 1-2 minutes, and by the time I'm ready to serve, the vegetables have cooked.

Vegetarians can substitute several "meaty" vegetables for the meat in my recipes, like portobello and shiitake mushrooms, butternut and other winter squashes, and eggplant; even thick slices of crusty chewy bread can work. When I use the term "meat" as a description, I'm referring to poultry, fish, and all livestock. In many of the vegetable entrées in this book, I combine rice with beans and legumes to create the complete protein—usually provided by meat—that our bodies require. However, our bodies use what we eat cumulatively and in concert over the course of the day, so that if you have rice for lunch or breakfast, you don't need it again at dinner. We need most of our protein and carbs during the day or when our bodies are using them, and fewer at night or when we're typically the least active. Consuming more of those foods early offers the opportunity to "work them off" as well.

Although I fully appreciate the importance of healthy eating, as a chef I don't believe in sacrificing flavor and texture to achieve it. I prefer most whole grain products on their own, but there are times when my taste has guided me to combine grains when cooking a meal, like brown and white rice, whole wheat and white pasta, and whole grain and white flour for a crusty peasant loaf, using 50 percent or more of the whole grains. At those times, I enjoy the extra depth of flavor, nutrients, and fiber provided by the whole grain products when tempered by the mild flavor and moist, comforting texture of the more refined ingredients.

❧

For those who currently want to change to a healthier diet, allow your taste buds time to get used to the new foods. You will first have to shed your present flavor preferences before you will appreciate the new; that will require patience, persistence, and friendly dialogue with yourself throughout the process. As you gradually wean yourself off of foods that aren't healthy, you might find the following suggestions helpful: if you add a lot of cream and/or sugar to your coffee and tea, begin to cut back on the amounts you use, a little at a time, until you become accustomed to the flavor, or try using milk and honey in place of the sugar and cream, also gradually cutting back on the amounts you use. For a sweet caffeinated alternative, heat unsweetened apple cider or juice with a cinnamon stick, pour it a third of the way up a large mug and fill the rest with boiling water and a teabag of your choice. If you drink soda, try instead to mix club soda or any type of plain sparkling water with unsweetened fruit juice (not from concentrate is best). Begin with a half and half mix and gradually cut back the juice to one-third or less. Always add the juice to the glass last; it will combine better with the water. These are alternatives you might find featured on a Neighborhood Café menu, as well as the "less" sweetened baked goods found in this book. If you bake at home, gradually cut the amount of sweetener that's called for in the recipes you typically use and substitute whole wheat pastry flour or "white whole wheat" flour for all, or at least half, of the white flour. If you bake bread at home, substitute at least half of the white flour with stone-ground, bread, or all-purpose whole wheat flour. If you eat a lot of jam with your bread, try instead mashing fresh or thawed berries in a small bowl with a little bit of honey. Use the mixture right away before the fruit exudes its juices, or, to make ahead of time, strain the lightly sweetened fruit after it releases its juices (about 20-30 minutes). Jar the fruit for up to 2-3 days in the refrigerator, and store juice separately, adding it to plain or sparkling water for an extra burst of flavor. For pb&j sandwiches, press thin slices of apple into the peanut butter or mash any sweet soft fruit with a fork (blackberries are my favorite), either in a small bowl or directly onto the peanut butter-covered slice.

If you love ice cream and eat too much of it, keep a container of sorbet in the freezer of the same or complementary flavor, like an orange sorbet to go with vanilla ice cream. Mix some of the sorbet into your bowl of ice cream – a little bit more each time coupled with smaller servings of ice cream – then begin stirring in a small amount of plain (preferably thick, low-fat Greek) yogurt; in this way, you end up cutting both the fat and sugar content of your treat.

Many whole grains have distinct flavors and possess a pleasant chewy texture when cooked. If you typically eat white enriched rice, you might need some time to get used to the new flavors and textures; keep a cooked, covered container of white rice in your refrigerator. When you prepare a whole hulled or cracked grain product like farro or bulgur (recipes in Chapter Eight), stir some of the rice (a little less each time) into the grains and heat before serving. Additionally, leftover whole and cracked grains make great salads when mixed with torn or baby greens, oil, vinegar or lemon, salt, and pepper – a prepared dish you might likely find at a Neighborhood Café.

If you love tortilla chips and eat too many, start accompanying them with thick bell pepper strips and radish halves, and/or celery boats and broccoli florets, progressively decreasing the number of chips you serve. These vegetables are crisp and make convenient vehicles to deliver salsa, guacamole, and other dips into your mouth. They also go well with hummus. Indeed, you might find an organic hummus or avocado and bean salsa plate with vegetable sticks and in-house baked corn tortilla or whole wheat pita chips on the menu at a Neighborhood Café (see recipe index).

I find potato chips tough to avoid; they're my number one weakness. I don't keep them in my house because they are the one food I find too difficult to resist. When at parties where they're served, I head straight for the bowl, or I resist them at first only to succumb to the craving before too long. I've stayed away from potato chips at home for so long that I hardly think about them anymore, but on those occasions when I do crave them I make my own baked chips (found in this book as a variation of Roasted Vegetables). If you have a similar challenge with potato chips and want to cut back on the amount you consume, try to substitute with less fat-intensive munchies like crunchy roasted chickpeas or fava beans, and wasabi peas.

Processed microwave popcorn is high in fat and often contains chemical additives; try making your own using just enough oil to lightly coat the bottom of a deep heavy-bottomed pan that has a lid. Begin to warm the oil over medium heat and add a single layer of corn kernels before the oil gets hot; cover the pan and raise the heat to medium-high. When the first kernel pops, lower the heat back to medium and move the pan back and forth over the burner. Once they start popping with frequency, lower the heat to medium-low, and, holding on to a handle with one hand and the lid with the other, keep the pan moving until the popping subsides. Turn off the heat, wait a minute or two, remove the lid carefully, and let the steam escape. Transfer the popped corn to a serving bowl, avoiding any burnt or unpopped kernels at the bottom of the pan. If you'd rather not make your own, try crushing into a bowl plain store-bought rice or popcorn cakes to the size of popcorn, toss them, or your homemade popped kernels, with well-oiled hands (or spray them with oil) until they're coated just well enough to adhere to seasoning; sprinkle with sea salt (and other spices to your taste). This is good finger food (if not too oily) to have in your car if you tend to snack while traveling, as are grapes, and a variety of fresh vegetables like juicy and crunchy romaine lettuce leaves, bell pepper and celery sticks, and baby carrots. They may help you to avoid an impromptu stop at a fast-food restaurant, as well.

If these suggestions don't sound appealing at first, I believe you will come to enjoy, and even prefer, at least some of these changes if you give them a try.

๛

Much of the above information in this chapter reflects my usual practices in the kitchen, for every cook has his or her way of doing things. Although keeping your kitchen surfaces and hands clean, and storing perishable foods unspoiled at safe temperatures remain universally important, most other kitchen practices are individual or passed down generationally. Although I like almost every food I can think of, I have many preferences, and I cook at home accordingly. However, when someone prepares a home-cooked meal for me, I leave those preferences behind, for I can hardly explain how much I appreciate whatever I'm being served. I feel honored when someone cooks for me.

Have fun in the kitchen!

Buckwheat Blueberry Muffins

Yield: 12 muffins

INGREDIENTS

Buckwheat flour | 1 cup
Whole wheat pastry flour | 1/2 cup
Sea salt | 1/4 tsp. plus 1/8 tsp.
Baking powder | 1-1/2 tsp.
Baking soda | 3/4 tsp.
Poppy seeds | 1-1/2 Tbsp.

Eggs | 2
Buttermilk | 1 cup
Extra virgin olive oil | 3 Tbsp.
Maple syrup | 1/4 cup
Unsweetened applesauce | 3/4 cup
Fresh or frozen unsweetened
    blueberries | 3/4 cup

DIRECTIONS

Grease muffin tin. In a bowl, mix the dry ingredients. Mix the wet ingredients in a separate bowl. Pour the wet into the dry, and stir gently from the bottom up until partially mixed; fold in blueberries until the ingredients are just combined. Fill each muffin cup almost to the top. Bake in a preheated 360-degree oven for 22-25 min., or until a knife through the center comes out clean and the top is springy to the touch.

Buttermilk Whole Grain Quick Bread
Yield: 1 – 9x5 loaf

Although this savory bread, and the Dark Rye Bread further along in the chapter are delicious on their own, on the menu at A Neighborhood Café, they could be used as vehicles for the following choices: butter and/or raw honey, sliced hard cheese along with fresh seasonal fruit, spreadable Neuchatel or goat cheese, housemade hummus, and mashed avocado with salt and pepper. A fresh, crunchy mix of chopped parsley and celery could be offered atop the avocado, hummus, and soft cheeses, as well.

INGREDIENTS

Whole wheat pastry flour (or "white whole wheat") | 1-1/2 cups
Stoned-ground whole wheat flour | 1-1/2 cups
Sea salt | 3/4 tsp.
Baking soda | 1 tsp.
Extra virgin olive oil | 1 Tbsp.
Egg, beaten | 1
Buttermilk | 1-1/2 cups
Fresh lemon juice | 1 Tbsp.
Maple syrup | 1 Tbsp.

DIRECTIONS

Grease and flour the loaf pan. Combine dry ingredients in a bowl. Stir in oil with a fork. Whisk remaining wet ingredients in another bowl, add to dry, and stir from the bottom up in a gentle folding motion until just blended. Pour into pan, and bake at 360 degrees for 40 min. Lower temperature to 325. Bake another 10–15 minutes. The center should feel firm and springy to the touch, and a knife through the center should come out clean. Cool 15 minutes, run the knife along the edges of the pan, and turn out onto a wire rack to cool.

VARIATIONS

Add 2 Tbsp. of sesame seeds, or 1 Tbsp. each of sesame and poppy seeds, to the dry mix.

Corn Bread

Yield: 1 – 9x5 loaf or 8" cast iron round or 9 muffins

*As a girl, I loved **"corn toasties,"** flat corn bread squares (found at that time in the supermarket freezer section) that I would pop in the toaster until hot and crispy. One day while fine-tuning this recipe for the book, instead of making a bread loaf or muffins, I spread the dough out as thinly as I could onto a lightly greased parchment-lined sheet pan, baked it at 400 degrees for 10 minutes, and cut them into squares after they had cooled. I was delighted with the first toasties I had eaten in decades, and when completely cool I froze the remaining ones for a quick treat or on-the-run breakfast. This method works using other muffin and quick bread batters as well.*

INGREDIENTS

Whole wheat pastry flour | 1/2 cup
Cornmeal | 1-1/2 cup
Sea salt | 1/2 tsp.
Baking powder and baking soda | 1 tsp. each
Egg | 1
Buttermilk | 1 cup
Maple syrup | 2-1/2 Tbsp.
Extra virgin olive oil | 1/4 cup

DIRECTIONS

Mix the dry ingredients together in a bowl. Make a well in the center. Lightly beat egg in another bowl, and whisk in remaining wet ingredients. Pour into the well, and mix the dry and wet ingredients with a fork until just blended (some lumps are OK). Pour batter into a greased pan; bake in a preheated 400-degree oven for 22-28 minutes. (12-15 for muffins), or until springy to the touch and a knife inserted into the center comes out clean.

Note: If you use a cast iron pan to bake the bread, lightly grease and preheat it before adding the batter.

Molasses Ginger Bran Muffins

Yield: 12 muffins and additional "toasties"

INGREDIENTS

Whole wheat pastry flour | 1-1/2 cups
Wheat bran flakes | 1-1/2 cups
Cornmeal or buckwheat | 1/2 cup
Baking soda | 2 tsp.
Sea salt | 1/2 tsp.
Ginger | 3 Tbsp. of finely chopped
   fresh (or 1-1/2 Tbsp. of dried)

Buttermilk | 2-1/2 cups
Eggs, beaten | 2
Unsweetened applesauce | 1/3 cup
Molasses | 1/2 cup
Maple syrup | 1/4 cup
Extra virgin olive oil | 3 Tbsp.
Currants | 1/2 cup
Walnuts, chopped (optional)| 1/3 cup

DIRECTIONS

Soak the bran and currants in 1 cup of the buttermilk; whisk together remaining dry ingredients in another bowl, and whisk the wet ingredients with the remaining buttermilk in the third. Gently mix wet into dry ingredients until partially blended. Add the soaked bran, currants, and the walnuts, if using, and fold batter until all ingredients are just combined. Spoon into greased muffin tin, each cup 2/3 full. For toasties, pour the remaining batter on a lightly greased parchment-lined sheet pan. Spread as thinly as you can into a rectangular shape. Bake in a preheated 350-degree oven, 10-12 minutes for toasties (should spring back to your touch), and 18–23 minutes for muffins. The top should spring back to your touch, and a knife inserted into the center of a muffin should come out clean. Allow both to cool; cut rectangle into toastable-sized squares. Freeze, and toast, as desired. This batter makes particularly good "toasties," as the molasses and currants caramelize in the toaster for an even richer flavor.

Note: A half recipe will yield 12 muffins or 1 pan of toasties.

Egg Bites

Yield: approximately 12

INGREDIENTS

Frozen chopped spinach, thawed and squeezed dry | 10 oz. pkg.

Oyster or shiitake mushrooms, halved and thinly sliced | 1/2 cup

Red bell pepper, chopped | 1/2 cup

Green onions, thinly sliced | 1/2 cup

Eggs | 8

Sea salt | 3/4 tsp. (cut to 1/2 tsp. or less if using particularly salty cheese)

Cayenne or Tabasco | 1/2 tsp.

Milk, not skim or 1% | 1/2 cup

Grated or crumbled cheese of choice | 1 packed cup

Russet potato, finely grated, rinsed, and squeezed dry | 1 (approximately 1-1/4 cup)

DIRECTIONS

Whisk together the eggs, salt, hot pepper, and milk. Stir in squeezed dry potato and spinach, oyster or shiitake mushrooms, green onion, bell pepper, and cheese; mix well. Fill muffin cups 2/3 – 3/4 of the way up in a well-greased muffin tin. Bake in a preheated 375-degree oven for approximately 18 minutes, or until slightly puffy and just set in the center. Serve them freshly baked, or cool thoroughly, cover, and refrigerate to enjoy within a few days; freeze for longer storage.

VARIATIONS

Substitute similar amounts of vegetables of your choice.

Add one or two slices of cubed whole wheat bread.

For a **frittata**, pour batter into a 9" round or square baking pan. Bake in a preheated 375-degree oven for approximately 35-40 minutes, or until just set in the center. Let cool 5 minutes before cutting.

Dark Rye Bread
Yield: 2 – 9x5 loaves

INGREDIENTS
Dark rye flour | 3 cups
Whole wheat flour | 1-1/2 cups
Baking powder | 4 tsp.
Baking soda | 1 tsp.
Sea salt | 2 tsp.
Caraway seeds | 1 Tbsp. plus 2 tsp.
Maple syrup and molasses | 2 Tbsp. each
Buttermilk | 2 cups

DIRECTIONS
Whisk together dry ingredients, including caraway seeds. Whisk sweeteners and buttermilk until blended, add to dry. Stir to form a soft dough. Pour into 2 greased loaf pans. Bake in a preheated 250-degree oven for 2-1/4 – 2-1/2 hours. The center should spring back to your touch, and a knife inserted there should come out clean. Allow to cool for 20 minutes before slicing. When completely cool, wrap and freeze 1 loaf, if desired.

OPTIONS
Replace rye flour with an equal amount of whole wheat flour, and omit or replace caraway seeds with 2 Tbsp. of poppy or sesame seeds, or 1 Tbsp. of each. Substitute the 2 Tbsp. of molasses with 1 Tbsp. of honey or 1 additional Tbsp. of maple syrup.

Lemon Pine Nut Cookie Thins

Yield: 1-1/2 dozen

INGREDIENTS

Whole wheat pastry flour | 1/3 cup

Sea salt | 1/4 tsp.

Zest and juice from lemon | 1 (zest from whole, juice from 1/2 or 1 Tbsp.)

Maple syrup | 1/4 cup

Egg | 1

Melted butter | 3 Tbsp.

Vanilla | 1-1/4 tsp.

Pine nuts (or chopped unsalted Brazil nuts) | 3 Tbsp.

DIRECTIONS

Whisk all the ingredients together in a bowl except for the nuts; stir in the nuts, cover, and refrigerate for one hour. Drop by teaspoons onto a parchment-lined baking sheet and spread each cookie to about 2 inches in diameter. Bake in a pre-heated 325-degree oven for 10-13 minutes until golden brown and slightly springy in the center.

VARIATIONS

For **Lemon Anise Cookie Thins**, add 3/4 tsp. of anise seeds to the dry ingredients.

Vegan 'Fruit of the Day' Cake
Yield: 1 - 8" round cake pan

INGREDIENTS
Whole wheat pastry flour | 1- 1/2 cups

Baking powder | 2 tsp.

Sea salt, cinnamon, and baking soda | 1/4 tsp. each

Unsweetened oat (or other alternative) milk | 1 cup minus 1 Tbsp.

Lemon juice | 1 tsp.

Maple syrup | 1/3 cup

Extra virgin olive oil | 3 Tbsp.

Fruit, such as pitted sliced apricots, peaches, cherries, or pears, berries (not strawberries), sliced kiwi | 2-1/4 cups

Nuts, finely chopped (optional) | 1/4 cup

DIRECTIONS
Mix dry ingredients in a bowl and wet ingredients in another bowl. Make a well in the center of the dry and pour in the wet ingredients; gently stir for a few strokes and then fold from the bottom up until almost combined, fold in the nuts, if using, until mixed in; some lumps are O.K. Pour the batter into a greased pan, cover top with the fruit, and press them slightly into the batter (alternatively, fold fruit into the batter when the wet and dry ingredients are nearly combined). Bake in a pre-heated 350-degree oven for approximately 40-55 minutes, or until a knife through the center comes out clean, and the top is springy to the touch and golden brown. If using fresh, not frozen fruit, check the cake after 35 minutes.

Savory Cheesy Muffins
Yield: 12 muffins

INGREDIENTS

Whole wheat pastry flour | 2-1/4 cup

Sea salt | 1/2 tsp.

Black pepper and thyme | 1/8 tsp. each

Baking powder | 1 Tbsp.

Eggs | 3

Extra virgin olive oil | 1 Tbsp.

Milk | 1-1/4 cups

Maple syrup | 2 Tbsp.

Parsley, green onion, and celery, finely chopped | 1/3 - 1/2 cup each

Cheddar, Gouda, or hard cheese of your choice, grated | 1-1/2 cups

Jalapeno peppers (optional), halved, seeded, and minced | 1-2

DIRECTIONS

Mix dry ingredients in a bowl. Lightly scramble eggs in another bowl, and whisk in the oil, milk, and syrup. Stir cheese, onion, and parsley into the flour mix. Add jalapenos, if using, or you can add 1/4-1/2 tsp. of cayenne. Make a well in the center, pour in the wet ingredients, and stir until just combined. Divide evenly between 12 greased muffin cups. Bake in a preheated 425-degree oven for 16-18 minutes, or until the tops are slightly puffy, golden, and springy to the touch.

Baked Apples
Yield: 4 or 8 servings

INGREDIENTS

Baking apples, like Rome Beauties or Granny Smith | 4
Zante currants | 1/4 cup
Hot water | 1/2 cup
White wine or water | 3 Tbsp.
Walnuts, ch. | 1/4 cup
Maple syrup | 2 Tbsp.
Sea salt | 1/8 tsp.
Vanilla extract | 1/2 tsp.
Cinnamon | 3/4 tsp.
Juice of fresh lemon | 1/2 (approx. 1 Tbsp.)
Butter | 1 Tbsp.

DIRECTIONS

Soak currants in water for 10-15 minutes. Meanwhile, mix the walnuts, syrup, vanilla, lemon, and seasonings in a bowl. Drain soaking liquid from currants into a 9" by 5" baking pan or other baking pan that holds the apples and allows for a little space between them. Stir wine (or water) into the liquid. Stir currants into stuffing mix. Leaving peel on the apples, remove the cores without going all the way through the apples. Stuff cavities with the currant mixture; place in the baking pan. Dot apples with butter, and bake in a preheated 375-degree oven for 40–50 minutes, or until tender when pierced with a knife, but firm enough to hold its shape.

VARIATIONS

Serve with Creamy Ginger Sauce (see recipe index).

Substitute Asian pears for the apples.

For a **vegan version**, use walnut or olive oil in place of the butter.

Basic Quick Bread, Muffin & Coffee Cake Mix
Yield: 1 – 9x5" loaf, 12 muffins, or one 8-9" round cake

INGREDIENTS

Whole wheat pastry flour | 2 cups
Baking powder | 4 tsp.
Baking soda| 1/2 tsp.
Sea salt | 1/3 tsp.
Cinnamon | 1/4 tsp. plus 1/4 tsp. for topping
Vanilla extract | 1 tsp.
Egg, beaten | 1
Maple syrup | 7 Tbsp. (1/2 cup minus 1 Tbsp.)
Buttermilk (or 3-1 ratio of plain yogurt and milk or water)| 1 cup
Extra virgin olive oil | 3 Tbsp.

DIRECTIONS

For **quick bread and muffins**, whisk together the dry ingredients in one bowl and the wet ingredients in another bowl. Add the wet to the dry mix, and stir gently in folding motion until just blended. A few lumps are fine. Divide evenly between greased muffin cups or pour into one greased loaf pan. Sprinkle with remaining cinnamon. Bake in a preheated 375-degree oven for approximately 16-20 minutes for muffins and 45-50 minutes for a loaf. A knife through the center should come out clean and the top should spring back to your touch.

VARIATIONS

Halfway through blending the wet and dry ingredients together, gently fold in 1-1/3 cups of berries (not strawberries), pitted and chopped nectarines or peaches, or pitted and halved cherries; increase baking time by approximately 5-10 minutes.

Add 1/3 cup chopped nuts or mixed seeds, and/or 1/2 cup of dried fruit (chop large pieces).

Substitute 1 cup of the flour with a 1/2 cup each of two of the following: cornmeal, oat bran, rye, or buckwheat.

For **Coffee Cake**: Omit cinnamon in the batter. Instead, combine 1/3 cup chopped nuts and 1-1/2 Tbsp. cinnamon in a small bowl; set aside. Fold 1-1/2 cups of berries (not strawberries), or cored 1/4" diced apple or pear, or thinly sliced pitted and quartered stone fruit into the muffin batter. Spoon half into a greased cake pan. Sprinkle with half the spice mix. Top with remaining batter and remaining spice mix. Bake at 375 degrees for approximately 40-50 minutes, or until a knife through the center comes out clean and the top springs back to your touch.

Raspberry Crisp
Yield: 1 – 8" square baking pan

TOPPING INGREDIENTS
Rolled oats and walnuts, chopped together | 1/2 cup each
Whole wheat pastry flour | 3/4 cup
Cinnamon | 3/4 tsp.
Sea salt | 1/4 tsp.
Zest from lemon | 1
Maple syrup | 1/3 cup
Cold butter, cut into small cubes | 2 Tbsp.

FILLING INGREDIENTS
Fresh or partially thawed frozen raspberries | approximately 3 cups
Maple syrup | 3 Tbsp.
Lemon juice | 1 tsp.
Sea salt and cinnamon | 1/8 tsp. each

DIRECTIONS
Combine the oats and walnuts, flour, salt, cinnamon, and zest from 1 lemon in a bowl. With a fork, stir in syrup to lightly coat the dry ingredients. Quickly, cut in the cold butter until it yields pea-size crumbles. In another bowl, toss raspberries with the next four ingredients. Slide into the greased pan and sprinkle with the topping to cover the fruit. Bake in a preheated 375-degree oven for 20 minutes, or until done. The top should be browned and the fruit cooked but retaining some of its shape.

VARIATIONS
For a **gluten-free version**, substitute the whole wheat flour for an equal amount of any combination of corn, oat, buckwheat, or chickpea flour.

For a **vegan version**, with a fork, stir 2 Tbsp. of walnut or olive oil into the flour mix instead of the butter.

For delicious **Raspberry Squares**, follow the mixing directions for the topping and filling as described above. Keep the topping chilled until ready to use. To the filling, partially mash the fruit; sift 2 tsp. whole wheat pastry flour through a strainer over the fruit, gently folding in one teaspoon at a time until blended. Press 2/3 – 3/4 of the topping mix in a thin layer evenly into the greased baking pan and top with the raspberry mixture. Sprinkle the remainder of the topping evenly over the fruit. Bake at 385 degrees for 30-32 minutes, or until the top is browned and raspberries are caramelized at the edges.

Sweet Potato Scones

Yield: 10 - 12

INGREDIENTS

Whole wheat pastry flour | 2 cups
Baking powder | 1 Tbsp.
Sea salt | 1/2 tsp.
Egg, beaten | 1
Maple syrup | 1/3 cup
Cold butter, cut into 12 pieces | 2 Tbsp.
Baked sweet potato, mashed | 1 cup

DIRECTIONS

Whisk the dry ingredients in a bowl; cut the butter into the mix. In another bowl, mix the syrup, egg, and sweet potato. Add to the dry mix, gently stirring and folding until just combined. Pat out on a floured surface to 1/2" thickness. Cut from end to end 1-1/2" crisscross diagonal lines for small classic diamond shapes (or 1-1/2-2" squares). Arrange close together on a greased baking sheet. Bake in a preheated 425-degree oven for 15-20 minutes, until golden brown and top springs back to your touch.

VARIATIONS

Substitute any winter squash, even canned pumpkin, for the sweet potato.

Peanut Butter Cookies
Yield: 1 dozen

INGREDIENTS
Salted, unsweetened peanut butter (creamy or chunky) | 1/2 cup
Maple syrup | 1/4 cup
Vanilla extract | 1/2 tsp.
Applesauce | 2 Tbsp.
Baking soda | 3/4 tsp.
Sea salt | 1/8 tsp.
Whole wheat pastry flour | 1/3 cup

DIRECTIONS
Combine peanut butter, syrup, vanilla, and applesauce in a bowl. Stir in baking soda and salt. Fold in flour until just blended. Divide into 12 equal pieces. Roll into balls. You might need to dust your hands lightly with flour (shake off the excess) for this task; the dough will be soft and sticky. Treat them like "hot potatoes;" the faster you work (with the least amount of fuss), at this point, the better. Place them on a parchment-lined ungreased sheet pan. Press down with the tines of a fork to get a crisscross pattern and to flatten the cookie to 2 - 2-1/4" in diameter. If needed, dip the fork in a bit of flour (shake off the excess) to prevent it from sticking to the cookies. Bake in a preheated 350-degree oven for 8-10 minutes. They will look underdone and feel a little dense in the center, but that's good! Let them cool at least 15 minutes.

VARIATION
Sprinkle the tops with sesame seeds before flattening them with a fork in a criss-cross pattern. Follow the same baking directions, as described above.

Note: This is a **vegan-compatible** recipe.

Dark Cocoa Muffins

Yield: 12 Muffins

INGREDIENTS

Dates, pitted and chopped or torn apart (preferably Medjool) | 1 cup

Water | 1 cup

Unsweetened cocoa powder | 3/4 cup

Baking soda | 1/2 tsp.

Sea salt | 1/4 tsp.

Room temperature butter and xv olive oil | 1 Tbsp. each

Vanilla extract | 1 tsp.

Eggs, beaten | 2

Maple syrup | 1/3 cup

Whole wheat pastry flour | 1/3 cup plus 1 Tbsp.

Cinnamon | 1 tsp.

Nutmeg | 1/2 tsp.

DIRECTIONS

Mix cinnamon and nutmeg in a small bowl. Combine water and dates in a sauce-pan. Bring to a boil, turn off the burner, and remove the pan from the heat. Cool slightly; mash until smooth with a potato masher (use a hand blender or food processor if you have one). Add cocoa, then butter and oil, and continue to mash to form a paste. Stir in salt, baking soda, syrup, and vanilla. Stir in egg until well combined and smooth. Gently fold in the flour until just blended. Spoon into greased muffin cups 2/3 of the way up, and sprinkle tops with the spice mix. Bake in a preheated 325-degree oven for 20-25 minutes, or until done. Top should just spring back to your touch, and a knife inserted into the center of a muffin should come out clean.

VARIATIONS

For **Dark Cocoa Cupcakes**, follow the above instructions, omitting spice mix. While they're baking, make the **cocoa frosting** by blending 1/3 cup unsweetened cocoa powder with 1/3 cup honey. Gradually, whisk in 2-1/2 Tbsp. soft butter until smooth and shiny. Frost the cupcakes after they've cooled.

For **Dark Cocoa Frosted Cake**, follow the recipe for dark cocoa muffins except pour the batter into a greased and floured (bottom and sides) 8" springform pan, and bake in a preheated 350-degree oven for approximately 20-25 minutes, or until a knife comes out clean from the center and the top is springy to your touch. When cool, run a knife along the edges of the pan and remove the side section of the pan. Lightly frost the top and sides of the cake. With a spatula, loosen the cake from the bottom of the pan and slide it onto a serving platter. Or more simply, bake in an 8" square pan; frost the top when cool, and cut servings directly from the pan.

Philip's Dark Chocolate Mousse
Yield: 8 servings

INGREDIENTS
Room temperature eggs, separated in 2 medium-size bowls| 4
Maple syrup or honey | 3 Tbsp. plus 2 tsp.
Good quality dark chocolate, 70-73 percent cocoa solids | 6 oz.
Butter | 1 Tbsp.
Vanilla extract | 1/2 tsp.
Sea salt | 1/16 tsp. (a pinch)

DIRECTIONS
Note: If you have an electric beater or kitchen aid it will make whisking the egg whites easier, but also easier to overbeat. Blending the beaten whites into the yolks when the peaks are almost stiff enough to hold their shape (the point just past soft peaks and just before stiff peaks) is my preference for texture and ease of combining the two mixtures.

Separate the egg whites and the yolks into two separate bowls. Add chocolate, vanilla, and butter to another bowl that fits over a pan that has lightly simmering water in it; the bottom of the bowl should not touch the water (and the bowl you use for the yolks should also fit over the simmering water without touching it). As soon as the chocolate mixture is nearly melted, remove the bowl to the counter and stir to combine. Add more water to the pan (but still below the level where the other bowl will sit), if necessary; bring back to a simmer, and lower the heat. Place the bowl with the egg yolks over the simmering water and whisk vigorously for 2 minutes. Continue whisking, slowly adding in 3 Tbsp. of the syrup or honey, until yolks are thicker in texture, slightly lighter in color, and reveal a trail mark left by the whisk. Remove from the heat, whisk for 1 more minute, and let cool to a close, but slightly warmer temperature than the chocolate. Blend the two mixtures together. In a clean bowl with a clean wire whisk, beat egg whites and salt until they're frothy and begin to thicken. Add the remaining 2 teaspoons of syrup

RECIPES

or honey and continue to whisk until the whites hold soft peaks when you lift the whisk. Continue whisking for 30 seconds to one minute longer or until just before (or as soon as) the peaks turn stiff. Lightly stir 1/4 of the whites into the yolk mixture. With a rubber spatula, delicately fold in the remaining whites, one-third at a time. It's OK to have a little egg white showing here and there; just gently break up the big clumps with your spatula. Spoon into a serving dish or individual bowls. Cover, and refrigerate for a few hours until set. The mousse is delicious on its own, but the recipe below for raspberry topping makes an excellent accompaniment.

VARIATION

For a more extravagant version, whip 1/2 cup of heavy whipping cream (not ultra-pasteurized) with 1-3/4 tsp. honey or maple syrup until you achieve soft peaks. Delicately fold into the mousse just as the last of the egg whites are almost blended in.

RASPBERRY TOPPING

Slightly mash 1-1/2 cups of fresh, or frozen and thawed, raspberries, leaving some berries whole. Gently stir in 3 Tbsp. of honey and mix until thoroughly combined (warm the honey lightly if needed for easier blending). Let the mixture sit for approximately 20-25 minutes, or until the berries release their juices. Mix well; spoon the sauce over one side of each serving of mousse; garnish with a sprig of mint.

CHAPTER 5

Worker-Owned Cooperatives and Cost Breakdowns

Although cooperative arrangements have existed for centuries, it wasn't until 1844 that the pioneers of Rochdale England (a group of 28 weavers and other skilled laborers) established the basic principles that define the modern-day cooperative movement. As noted by Jennifer Wilhoit on the cultural-survival.org website, "entrepreneurs who had previously been capable of the sustainable production of high-quality goods found themselves competing with large industries that sold less-expensive, poorly made products." These disparities in size and production became a "driving force in their decision to move toward cooperation." With the rise of consumer demand for cheaper, more plentiful goods, many of those large industries relied on degrading labor practices to meet the quotas mass production demanded: "Employees lost control over working conditions; low pay, long hours, unsanitary workplaces, and no mechanisms for claiming worker rights added to the growing frustration among laborers." The International Cooperative Alliance was formed in 1895 by E. V. Neale and Edward Greening, who felt that a worldwide organization could support the mission of employee-owned businesses and help promote their continued existence. The alliance remains a force today.

Cooperatives now range in type, size, and function. There are producer co-ops, such as the Montana Organic Producers Co-op, Texas Organic Cotton (and Food Crop) Marketing Cooperative, and Organic Valley, where producers combine resources to market their products. There are also purchasing cooperatives, such as Amicus Solar Cooperative, where businesses pool resources to better compete with large companies and chains. The most common cooperatives are consumer-based. They're owned by the people using the services, as in Credit Unions, or by those purchasing goods, such as REI and many local health food stores. This system could potentially work for a Neighborhood Café.

But the worker cooperative perhaps best represents the model for a Neighborhood Café. According to the National Cooperative Business Association, members of worker cooperatives are both employees and owners, the businesses they create democratically controlled by their members and not by outside investors. They can be new business start-ups, as well as conversions of existing businesses. As noted by the Nebraska Cooperative Development Center, the numerous entity options such businesses can assume include sole proprietorship, general partnership, limited partnership, limited liability partnership, limited liability company, "S" and "C" corporations. They all possess different advantages, disadvantages, and their own set of legal requirements. A breakdown of these structures can be found on the NCDC website. I specifically want to add "B" and "Benefit" corporations to the above list of business options because their bylaws represent Neighborhood Café values better than any other type of corporation. Growing in number over the past decade in the United States, benefit corporations possess a business structure shaped by a commitment to consider positive impacts on workers, the community, and the environment, in addition to their for-profit goal. Authorized by only 35 states and the District of Columbia, I find it difficult to understand why a state would not approve the legal status of a company wanting to make an open commitment to the growth of their local communities and the protection of their workers and our shared environment. It seems to me that there are enough customers who would support such models given the choice and, in turn, would make it profitable for those "brands" (and their stockholders) associated with more ethical goals. B corporations (or B corps) are different. They have no legal status but have a third-party certification granted by B Lab, a global non-profit organization that recognizes and scores the company's commitment to certain sustainable practices.

On another site, www.consciouscompanymedia.com, Rachel Zurer describes the differences between cooperatives overseen by managers and others that possess an elected board of directors and board president. Although such figures "mak[e] strategic decisions and hav[e] operational authority, they are empowered by and responsible to the full membership." Each member of a worker-owned cooperative has "one equal share of the business; they have one equal vote, whatever their position, seniority or pay." Ms. Zurer goes on to describe some smaller worker-co-ops that have no internal hierarchy at all; decisions, as well as tasks, are delegated to individuals or groups.

Depending on the chosen structure of the cooperative, the employee-owners can be paid wages and benefits as employees and also share in the profits as co-owners. They decide with their votes what percentage of the profits go back into the business, and what percentage becomes the "patronage" dividend, which represents the share of profits each member receives at the end of the year, a figure often based on hours worked. As well, an individual member's liability depends on the chosen form of the cooperative and can be limited to the amount of money that the member invests, and no more, as in limited liability companies.

My preference for worker-owned cooperatives has developed from my own business experience and personal background. My awareness of cooperative businesses during my working years was primarily limited to the health food store retail co-ops I frequented and, later on, the Humboldt Creamery producer cooperative, which met with an unfortunate end because of alleged dishonest management and proven loan fraud. Although I have only participated in sole-proprietorships and a general partnership in the past, and even though I've been fortunate with the individuals I've employed, my business experiences have taught me the value of having workers invested in the business. Although challenges abound in democratically run businesses or when operating by consensus, I think the benefits enjoyed by working together towards a common goal for the good of both the company and the community far outweigh the drawbacks. Obstacles confront all types of businesses, so why not choose a format that promotes equality and empowerment, where the outlay of starting and operating costs, as well as potential losses, are shared by all involved? I recognize, of course, that such a system might not appeal to everyone. Creating the organizational structure within which you will be most comfortable remains the most important consideration when starting a business.

The following organizations have informative websites, which may contain legal and technical assistance to parties interested in starting a worker-owned Neighborhood Café or other cooperative business: Grassroots Economic Organizing, Nebraska Cooperative Development Center, Green Worker Cooperative Co-op Academy in N.Y., Federation of Southern Cooperatives Land Assistance Fund in Alabama, and Mondragon Cooperative Corporation in Spain (one of the world's most successful network of worker cooperatives). In addition, the Ohio Employee Ownership Center has generated, in collaboration with the United Steelworkers Union and Mondragon, a template for how "union co-ops" can function, while the Democracy at Work Institute, in partnership with the University of Wisconsin, has produced a helpful case study, "Successful Cooperative Ownership Transitions". Many of the businesses listed below are featured in that report.

Co-ops are gaining in popularity throughout the United States and around the world as more and more blue-collar workers and campesino/as find themselves adversely affected by the financial structures that now dominate the global economy. Montana Organic Producer Co-op's website highlights the struggle smaller farms confront when competing with the corporate food giants: "We believe that collaboration between farmers, instead of competition, is the key to the salvation of the independent family farm in the U.S." I'm convinced that applies as well to independent family farms, and other small businesses, around the globe.

The beauty of cooperative businesses lies in the relationship between the companies' own best interests and the best interests of the communities in which they operate. As Jennifer Wilhoit argues, "Cooperatives do not operate in isolation from their community, but are integrated into society. Some offer various types of educational opportunities to non-members; others support local projects benefiting their communities." Ideally, cooperative members enjoy a greater resiliency during hard times because they're built on a solid foundation of cooperation and strength in numbers. The cooperative movement's importance lies in the profound cultural shift it represents, as Marjorie Kelly states in YES! magazine, which "doesn't arise from government action, or protests in the streets, but from within the structure of our economy itself. Not from the leadership of a charismatic individual, but from the longing in many hearts, the genius of many minds, the effort of many hands to build what we know, instinctively, that we need."

Whether or not starting or joining a cooperative business appeals to you, the stories behind the companies listed below should inspire and encourage readers to explore alternative business visions of what our future economy can look like:

1. Evergreen Cooperatives, Cleveland, OH
2. Isthmus Engineering, WI
3. Bob's Red Mill, OR
4. Alvarado Street Bakery, CA
5. Rainbow Grocery, CA
6. Ithaca Health Alliance, N.Y.
7. Blue Scorcher Bakery Café, OR
8. A Yard and a Half Landscaping Cooperative, MA
9. The New Moon Café, WA
10. Mondragon Worker Cooperative Corporation, Basque, Spain

Whether a Neighborhood Café operates as a cooperative or other for-profit business, or a non-profit organization, it can benefit the community in many ways. The Café could model itself after The Grange, which, during its heyday in the late nineteenth and early twentieth centuries, promoted cooperative and community values. The Grange (officially referred to as The National Grange of the Order of Patrons of Husbandry) was organized in Washington, D.C. in 1867. It promoted interest in cooperative activities, including group purchasing. Grange halls often contained libraries, and they encouraged reading, as well as conversation and debates on subjects of interest to members. Granges served as adult education resources for numbers of people. Many of these halls became centers for food, clothing, and supply distribution for those who had lost their homes during natural disasters. Cultural changes over time, involving insurance laws, the growing importance of television, and the decline of farming, contributed to the diminishing role of The Grange across the country. There are under-utilized and closed grange halls all across our nation.

A Neighborhood Café could also play host to out-of-town guests and community residents from different walks of life. They could speak about the culture within which they grew up and how those cultures still live in their food, music, education, and family values (perhaps alternating those talks with movie nights depicting these cultures). "Different walks of life" would also include neighbors from a variety of economic and social circles. The more we learn about each other as a human community (especially while in a safe, open environment), the less we will fear and judge one another, and the more we will come to understand how our own cultural identity and personal experiences shape us.

There exists an endless supply of creative ideas that can move us forward towards more cooperation, goodwill, and good humor. One such ingenious idea took form over a decade ago at a Staten Island restaurant in New York City called Enoteca Maria, where grandmothers or "Nonnas" create lunch and dinner menus. It began with Italian grandmas and has expanded to include any "Nonna" cooking her favorite dish from the country of her origin. Trip Advisor has rated the restaurant with 4.5 out of 5 stars and awarded the restaurant its Certificate of Excellence. This type of concept can serve a community café or restaurant well, providing an excellent way to enhance the lives of those senior citizens who preserve the traditions of "home-style" fare, and the customers who benefit from the knowledge and enjoyment of those traditions. In Enoteca Maria's case, the Nonnas receive little or no salary, but a monthly vote by participants crowns the "Nonna Chef" who wins a gift card from a local retailer.

On a smaller scale, when my partner, Joe, and I owned our restaurant, "Squisi's," we created "guest chef" nights. We would pay local chefs (and one friend brought in from out-of-town), as well as a few nonprofessionals, to come in and cook their own food. They would supply the menu and a list of ingredients needed, while we would place the orders and promote the event locally. The chefs - usually with a helper or two they brought with them - prepped and cooked the dinners. On these occasions, we sat down and enjoyed the experience of being customers in our own restaurant. One evening our featured "guest" was our waitstaff; Joe and I waited tables while our staff cooked. Those evenings provided big fun for everyone involved, staff, guest chefs, our customers, and Joe and me.

❧

The cost breakdowns for food businesses remain similar for all types of business formats, cooperative or not. Restaurants and cafés are invariably high overhead businesses: they require more than average expenses to operate, as well as to start. Having worked in the restaurant business for many decades, I must confess that they are indeed labors of love. Their success rate hovers close to our national divorce rate at approximately 45%, which makes both restaurants and marriages risky propositions. They both require long-term commitments, attention to detail, good communication skills, hospitable environments, and careful maintenance. Yet people will continue to open restaurants as they will continue to marry - and work hard in both cases to make them work.

Start-up costs involve a variety of expenditures, including payments for rental security deposits, licenses, inspections and fees, equipment and furnishings, initial inventory costs for food, beverage, and supplies, and operating expenses to see you through your first four to six months of operation. These costs should be estimated early on in order to have a clear picture of the finances you'll need to procure before you move ahead with your business venture.

As I searched for up-to-date information on current cost breakdowns, I found those numbers pretty much the same as many years ago when I last needed such information. Running a restaurant involves a variety of expenditures, as well, including costs for food and beverage, labor, and fixed operating expenses such as rent, utilities, insurance, fees, advertising, and services for payroll and accounting. All, of course, must add up to less than your total revenue.

Food and labor costs are calculated as a percentage of total sales. If a café brings in $5,000 per week in sales, and the total cost of food and beverages is $1,450 for that week, then the food cost is 1450 divided by 5000, or 29 percent. If at the same restaurant, labor (which includes payroll taxes and benefits) costs $1,600 for the week, then the labor cost is 1600 divided by 5000, or 32 percent.

According to author Steven Buckley, on the website smallbusiness.chron.com, "Certain fast food restaurants can achieve labor cost as low as 25 percent, while table service restaurants are more likely to see labor in the 30 percent to 40 percent range, depending on the menu and extensiveness of service. Food costs (including beverages) for the restaurant industry run typically from the 28 percent to 35 percent range, depending upon the style of restaurant and the mix of sales."

When pricing an item on your menu to reflect a food cost within that range, first figure out the total cost of goods required to produce the finished menu item, meaning every ingredient in the recipe. Triple that total, and adjust the number a little higher or lower according to what the market will bear and what you feel is fair. After each menu item is similarly calculated, you want the average to reflect a sustainable food cost percentage.

As a general guideline, food and labor costs together should be in the 60 percent to 65 percent range. If one number falls on the high side, the other must be on the low to stay within the parameters for profitability. That means your remaining operating expenses must come in under 35-40 percent, depending on your combined food and labor cost. According to yourbusiness.azcentral.com (part of the USA Today network), "The typical restaurant operates on a slim profit margin of 2-6 percent," which represents what remains after you deduct your total operating expenses from your gross revenue. In your written business plan, I recommend estimating your total costs on the high side, your sales projections on the low, and include a percentage value (at least 5%) for unexpected costs. You will need to write out a list of all initial expenditures as well, like deposits, permits, insurance, and beginning inventory. If, after you've considered all expenses, the numbers look good and the business can pay all workers or worker-owners (including your salary), you can then think of reinvesting a larger percentage of the profit back into the business, which would decrease your tax liability at the same time. Owning a business requires capital to make improvements and maintain everything in good working order; our tax code allows you to write off some of those expenditures.

Factors to consider if your food costs become prohibitive are food and beverage waste, pricing, portion sizes, theft, and excessive "comps" (giving product away without charge). If your labor costs remain too high, you may want to adjust hours and job descriptions that will enhance fair, yet common sense productivity goals. Keep in mind, however, that staff time will be required to contribute to the Neighborhood Café's Information Center. To increase profits, you might consider producing or bringing in higher margin products to sell, and perhaps charging a small commission on sales from the local art you feature.

If your final numbers do not reveal a profit, consider instead a lower overhead business that might allow you to reach your goals. Perhaps you could start with a Neighborhood Café food truck or vendor stall at a local farmer's market (in the craft area, usually separate from the farmers), or you could occupy a space inside an existing business or institution. You might contact a local elected official and the property owner of a long-closed storefront or big box store in your neighborhood, which might present an opportunity to obtain a long-term lease (with a one year option to renew on your end) that includes both reduced rent and tax breaks in return for implementing minor upgrades to the property.

If I haven't yet scared you away from the prospect of opening a café, our recent pandemic history might tip the scale. I wrote this chapter before the Covid pandemic began in early 2020, and after the last two tumultuous years I don't know what the future holds for cafés and restaurants; some evolution surely must take place. Many restaurants were unable to survive such a prolonged disruption to their income. Hopefully, the health and safety protocols we learned to put in place during this crisis might help mitigate damage in future outbreaks. Now in its third year, the pandemic has contributed to increased costs and demand for materials and labor. At the same time, accelerating climate-related conditions are putting an additional strain on our agricultural and economic health. However, I do not doubt that we can develop strategies (possibly spawned at a Neighborhood Café) that will help us live with, or overcome, these challenges. The foodservice industry will certainly have to transform itself in light of the threats presented by these persisting global crises.

CHAPTER 6

Sweets; Assessing Whole and Refined Grains and Sugars

In my early twenties, I used all my savings to backpack through Europe - my first time abroad. With airline tickets from New York to Athens and Paris to New York, I intended to work my way slowly north and west from Greece to France. Those plans quickly changed in Athens when I met two young women from British Columbia whose company I greatly enjoyed. A cold winter came as an unwelcome surprise, so when Anne and Elizabeth invited me to go south to Israel with them I jumped at the opportunity. We stayed for three months, working for room and board at a Moshav in a stunning area in the eastern region of the Sinai Peninsula on the Red Sea coast. A Moshav resembles a Kibbutz, but instead of the communal sharing of all resources, residents in the former can maintain their own possessions as well. After working, cavorting, and snorkeling there for two and a half months, we left that magical place to continue our travels, Anne and I exploring outlying areas for a week or two before going our separate ways. Anne loved chocolate and every day at around 1:00 p.m. she would eat a chocolate bar. Wanting, of course, to be sociable, I happily joined her in this daily ritual. The years have blurred many of my memories of this trip, but I remember clearly the first midday on my own again. Walking through the streets of the small village where we had parted, all of a sudden I experienced an overwhelming desire for a chocolate bar. I looked up at the town clock and, sure enough, it was 1:00. The vision I had of eating a chocolate bar was so vivid, the urge so compelling, that it prompted me to stop and take notice. Should I indulge this desire? Would that mean I would need a chocolate bar every day at 1:00? I decided not to succumb to this bullying urge.

For me, that experience perfectly illustrates both the physical and mental addictiveness of sweets. While I enjoy celery and lettuce and eat them daily, they never attract me as powerfully as did that 1:00 bar of chocolate. I do, however, allow myself some addictions: I have coffee every morning and one to two glasses of wine with most dinners. I'm certainly not one to preach to others about avoiding sugar. But I want to encourage a moderate intake, and (with accompanying recipes) a switch from mainstream and mass-produced candy and baked goods, to sweets that have more nutritional value. I much prefer cooking to baking, but the challenge to develop and fine-tune recipes for confections that are, for the most part, healthful, yet taste like they're not, has inspired me as a baker.

I first tried my hand at baking as a teenager. I made an excellent cheesecake (thanks to Better Homes and Gardens), baked my mom's lemon and chocolate chiffon pies, and prepared the Christmas cookies that I gave as gifts for several years. The cookies I chose to make came from a Pillsbury cookie booklet. Before I adopted this new hobby, I was stricken with a case of acne so horrid that it landed me at a dermatologist's office. I received infrared treatments and was sent home from the first visit with a long list of what I couldn't eat if I was serious about ever looking like a cool teenager again. I stopped drinking soda, eating fried foods, and indulging in sweets until my face cleared.

Because I had forsaken sugar for what felt like ages, when I started baking and following published recipes, everything tasted too sweet to me. I began experimenting with reduced amounts of sugar and ended up with the formula that I use to this day. With most recipes, cutting the sugar by a third (sometimes only by a quarter) will create a product that remains sweet, but not so sweet that it dominates the other ingredients. With my confidence high, I then began replacing white flour with whole grain versions that had more flavor and nutrients, providing a greater depth to the final product.

Today, a great number of scientific studies confirm that sugary foods and drinks not only contribute to tooth decay but increase the risks of a multitude of health issues. Sugar's negative impact on health can accumulate slowly over the years; the body also responds poorly when digesting refined and enriched white flours and grains. Without the whole food nutrients, fiber, and complex carbohydrates present in whole grains, the body processes refined starches much like it does refined sugars, by using its reserves of vitamins, minerals, and enzymes to break them down into usable sugars for fuel. The body needs the fiber that is present in whole grains and fruits to slow digestion that, in turn, keeps insulin levels from spiking.

Fresh fruits and modest amounts of unsweetened dried fruits are the best sources of fructose; both represent excellent sources of fiber, nutrients, and antioxidants. Superior sources of sugar, in general, come from nutrient-dense whole foods like vegetables, including legumes and beans, and whole, sprouted, and partially cracked grains, that are each bound in networks of fiber that decelerate digestion and limit rapid increases in blood sugar.

Even though the body processes raw honey, molasses, and maple syrup as added sugars, they nonetheless provide some nutrients, as opposed to nutritionally void table sugar; moreover, smaller quantities of honey and maple syrup achieve the same degree of sweetness as white sugar. Since raw honey loses many of its trace nutrients when exposed to high heat, I typically save its use for cold, warm, and room temperature foods. I don't use much molasses, since it's a by-product of white granulated sugar, and an increase in the demand for molasses might lead to an increase in the production of white sugar. As much as I can, I use fresh, frozen, or stewed fruit to sweeten batters or highlight most desserts. When I do use maple syrup, I find the extra cost mitigated because I use less sweetener. Additionally, many health food stores carry the syrup in bulk, making it more affordable. If the cost is still too high, use honey instead. If you'd like to use pure maple syrup or honey to replace the sugar in a recipe, cut the amount by about a third in most cases.

In developing the following recipes, I sought finished products that contained more wholesome ingredients than most baked goods, yet were still sweet-tooth satisfying. However, if you're used to highly sugared sweets, please allow your taste buds and body to adjust to the change. My first round of Christmas cookies, given to my brother Phil decades ago, elicited a, "Thanks, sis, but they're not sweet enough." Today, he reduces the sugar in a recipe when he bakes, and much prefers the resulting flavors. If you bake frequently at home you might want to reduce the sugar gradually, perhaps starting with a quarter less and, after a month or so, moving to a third less. When you come across a recipe that doesn't require much sweetener, use your judgment and cut back by a smaller amount or leave it alone.

Sugar addiction remains an important topic, challenging to tackle because our culture revolves around sweets throughout the year. Valentine's Day, Easter, Mother's Day, Halloween, and Christmas all represent holidays that encourage the consumption of sugar. Girl Scout cookie drives and bake sales depend, of course, on the marketing of sweets, but candy, pastries, cookies, and cakes can also be found at office meetings and church socials, in omnipresent vending machines, ubiquitous commercials, down the aisles in grocery and drug stores and at their check-out stands where you can't walk away or distract your children long enough to escape their notice. All of these holidays, communal activities, and businesses thrust sugar into our, our children's, and our grandchildren's faces, every day and everywhere.

Most people in this country love sweets, and many are addicted to sugar, precisely because the more sugar one eats, the more one wants. Similar processes drive the desire for highly processed and fast foods, as well as snacks that are high in salt and fat, and low in fiber. These foods are typically high in poor quality carbohydrates and calories. Our body's survival mechanisms are designed to want high caloric foods, and carbohydrates produce increased serotonin, which helps relieve stress. However, we can enjoy a more sustainable reduction in stress levels when we reduce our consumption of those foods and take pleasure in a diet rich in whole grains and beans, fresh fruits and vegetables, and moderate amounts of other nutrient-dense carbohydrates, like nuts and seeds.

Today, the big businesses that deal in fast foods, the refining of sugar, and commercial grain commodities, are huge power brokers that often prioritize their growth over our health. In all fairness, we have much more knowledge today of the basics of nutritional science than we had in years past. The beginnings of commercial milling came about, in fact, from the desire not only to produce more, but to prolong the shelf life of grains by removing the oils present in the bran and germ (which house the nutrients and fiber, but go rancid with prolonged storage). Medical professionals did not fully recognize the harmful effects that sustained consumption of refined grains and added sugars can cause until only a few decades ago. However, now that we possess a better understanding of the science behind healthy nutrition, it is past time to change the "business as usual" model that drives the food industry to advertise the need and create the desire for the unhealthy foods that flood the market. This won't change until we call for it to change.

We could encourage a shift in the food distribution network by asking for more whole food choices, not only on market shelves but at deli counters, food chains, cafeterias, street food vendor carts and stalls. We need to replace processed foods with affordable options like baked white and sweet potatoes with healthy fixins, grilled corn-on-the-cob on a stick, spiced al dente brussels sprouts and squash, fava beans, peanuts, and chestnuts roasted in their shells or pods, refreshing slices of watermelon and other fruits, like strawberries (healthy even when dipped in dark chocolate). Whole wheat pitas stuffed with spinach and cheese, warmed until melted and drizzled with (optional) raw honey, can make a quick satisfying snack or light meal. As well, offerings such as lightly-oiled grilled eggplant, peppers, onions, and mushrooms with beans, greens, pickled radish, cheese, salsas, and savory yogurt dressings, make delicious stuffings for whole grain versions of flatbreads, rolls, pizza crusts, tortillas, and rice paper, or enticing toppings for "whole grain" bowls.

As we wean ourselves from the excessive intake of overly refined flours, grains, and sugars, and additive-filled and other unwholesome foods, our buying habits will change, which will, in turn, drive the processed food manufacturers to follow suit. We have already begun to change their direction slowly. Today, for instance, bakers can choose from a far greater range of products than when I first began in the food industry. Whole wheat pastry flour, "white whole wheat" (made from soft spring wheat), and other whole grain flours, are milled finer to yield lighter baked goods and "all-purpose" versatility. Although fine-milling reduces their nutrient and fiber content, they still retain more nutritive value than flours that are stripped of their bran and germ. Other processed foods contain more whole grains now, fewer refined sweeteners, salts, and trans fats. Still, progress in producing healthier foods remains slow, often hampered by misleading labels and advertisements.

I enjoy reading food labels, and I can spend hours in a grocery store doing just that. It's one of my comfort zone activities, a walking meditation like Tai Chi; I shed thoughts of all else and get lost in the activity. That said, I realize most people don't have the time or inclination for such an endeavor, and they often get frustrated when trying to sort out the detailed information on each label. Others don't bother to attempt such a time-consuming and confusing task. For some, that reason is a lack of trust in the integrity of our food labeling system and the companies that influence that system. However, even given insufficient oversight and the possible inaccuracies on a nutritional panel that the FDA legally allows, I still find it a useful guide. When coupled with the ingredients list, it remains the best way a consumer can determine the attributes of a product. Additionally, the more familiar we become with food labels as they are now, the better able we'll be to direct the changes we want made to them.

Analyzing the nutritional information on labels often led me to wonder why some whole grain products were high in fiber content while others were not; it didn't make sense to me. After researching this topic, I was able to come away with a general impression as to why. In 1999, a definition of "whole grain" was created by the American Association of Cereal Chemists (AACC) International, an organization of food industry professionals and scientists. Seven years later, this definition was adopted by the US Food and Drug Administration. It states that "whole grain refers to any mixture of bran, endosperm, and germ in the proportions one would expect to see in an intact grain." In a 2013 Scientific America article by Melinda Moyer, she explains that "the grains can be, and usually are, processed so the 3 parts are separated and ground before being incorporated into foods...Some processing techniques have been shown to degrade natural antioxidants and reduce fiber content. In fact, the AACC Intl. recently proposed modifying its definition of "whole grain" to allow for some nutrient losses during processing." Additionally, the FDA requires that only 51 percent or more whole grains be present for the company to claim the product as "whole grain". Moyer concludes by saying, "Compared with intact whole grains, though, processed whole grains often have lower fiber and nutrient levels", and she recommends that people cook with intact whole grains as much as they can. Deborah Angersbach, Doctor in Naturopathic Medicine, explains, "The whole grain is processed very differently by our bodies than [the ground product]: [milled grain] releases the starches to be absorbed a lot more quickly which then raises blood sugars a lot faster than if we have to break down the outside of the grain ourselves and slowly release the starch inside." In other words, although we are getting more nutrients from whole grain flours than from their white flour counterparts, they no longer possess their whole food integrity. This describes one reason why processed foods and baked goods made with flours of any kind (including gluten-free flour and starch mixes) are best eaten in modest amounts.

Other information I consider when choosing a product is also found on the ingredients list and nutritional facts statement. As an example, if sprouted wheat berries or other sprouted grains are listed, I know they were milled from intact grains since only whole grains sprout; this affirms the grains weren't processed into separate components and later recombined. Additionally, some products with a certified "whole grain" stamp on their label could still be high in added sugars, fats, salts, and other additives I look to avoid. In the end, I primarily buy whole, sprouted, and cracked grain products that are high in fiber, and low in added sugars, sodium, and fats, especially saturated fats. Although food labels should certainly be improved, at present they're the most useful tool a consumer has to identify the overall quality of a processed product. Labeling laws require serious updating, with full disclosure privileged over misrepresentation through clichés that possess little meaning, like "all natural" and "healthy choice." It's important to support consumer advocacy groups that have our best interests at heart, and help them succeed in making truth in advertising a reality for us and our children.

The vulnerability of our children is particularly apparent on holidays like Halloween, which depend on the aggressive marketing of sweets. As a mother, I always had mixed feelings about Halloween. I didn't want to deprive my son of the pleasure involved in masquerading as his favorite character while trick-or-treating, yet I resented Danny's exposure to such a voluminous amount of candy. A few years ago, I twice went to see the Disney film "Coco," once on my own to judge its appropriateness (lots of skeleton ghosts in the previews) for my, then, six-year-old granddaughter, and a second time with Ruby; we both appreciated such a beautifully told tale and delightful sensory experience; it was so much fun! The film also taught me more about the origins of our own Halloween, The Day of the Dead, when people in other cultures celebrate deceased family members and loved ones, displaying their photographs, reminiscing, lighting candles, playing music, and enjoying a fiesta table prepared with both savory dishes and sweets.

I believe we should reform our Halloween so that it becomes more representative of its parent holiday. The day would call on us to honor with stories of the past our ancestors and friends who have died, all while enjoying good food, music, dancing, children playing in their costumes, and trick-or-treating, too. Treats don't have to lack nutritional value: small boxes of raisins, little bars of dark (preferably at least 70% cacao content) chocolate, either plain or with nuts and fruits, can both taste good and be nutritionally responsible. There are many "no candy" options as well. Many dollar stores sell packages of mini Play-doh containers, rubbery prehistoric animals, craft supplies, party favors, and shiny sparkly things that appeal to children as much if not more than candy. What ideal can you imagine for a Halloween celebration, and what would you do to make that happen?

We have the power to recreate every holiday similarly, every office and church social, every bake sale, fund-raiser, and lemonade stand. Only we, as individuals, have the power to do that, to recreate our present, and thus our future, until enough individuals join in and re-create society.

Authentic Lemonade
Yield: 2 quarts

Although the drink has been a worldwide favorite for many years, lemonade stands are part of our cultural heritage and possibly the first income earned for many children across the country. The original stands offered glasses of lemonade made from freshly squeezed lemons, water, and sweetener, selling typically for three cents to a nickel. By the time I set up my first lemonade stand, fresh lemons were beginning to be replaced by frozen concentrate, which I sold for a quarter per disposable cup. You can still find stands that offer the real thing, or that use unsweetened concentrate. However, too often these days, after paying my fifty to seventy-five cents, I receive a drink made from a powdered mix that I consider only faintly reminiscent of the naturally tart fruit, and which has a lingering chemical aftertaste. The following recipe yields a drink similar to what I remember lemonade tasting like as a child.

INGREDIENTS

Juice of fresh lemons* | 8-10 (1 cup of juice)
Water | 4-1/2 cups
Raw honey | 3/4 cup
Lemon, sliced thinly | 1

DIRECTIONS

Warm 1 cup of the water; pour into a serving pitcher. Add the honey and stir well until completely blended. Add remaining (cold) water and lemon juice. Stir until well mixed. Stir in lemon slices, and chill.

VARIATIONS

Use Meyers lemons, and cut the amount of honey by half, or to taste.

Use a mix of lemons and limes for a delicious citrus-ade. If you add oranges as well, cut the amount of sweetener you use.

If you're making large quantities and don't want to juice so many lemons, buy unsweetened frozen lemon juice concentrate, reconstitute with water according to label directions, and substitute that mix for the fresh juice. Or better yet, use a half and half mix of reconstituted concentrate and fresh juice or even a 2/3–1/3 or 3/4–1/4 mix. Try to use some fresh lemons and lemon slices.

*Note: To get the most juice from a lemon with help only from a fork, roll a whole lemon on the counter using some pressure from your hands (this will break some of the inner membranes and help release more juice once cut open). Halve the lemon, and with a fork, over a bowl, stab midway through the center of one of the halves. Turn the fork with one hand as you twist the lemon in the opposite direction, squeezing all the juice into the bowl; remove the pits with the fork. A medium-sized lemon yields approximately 2 Tbsp. of juice, or 2 lemons for 1/4 cup.

Refreshing Juice Sodas

INGREDIENTS

Unflavored club soda, seltzer, or sparkling mineral water
Unsweetened fruit juice (preferably not from concentrate)
Ice (optional)

DIRECTIONS

Put a small amount of ice in a glass, pour the sparkling water almost to 2/3 of the way up, and top with the juice of your choice.

You can start with a half and half mixture of juice and club soda if you're used to highly sweetened soft drinks, and work your way to a 2/3-1/3 mix or even a 3/4–1/4 mix.

VARIATION: EGG CREAM

Before and after WW2 my grandpa Saul started several business ventures within a two-block radius in Harlem. With my grandma Mary helping him, the first business I remember was an ices store – a storefront really - where he prepared his grape variety using a bit of red wine to give it an extra boost of flavor. "Egg Creams" (eggs are not one of the ingredients) were popular in N.Y.C. back then, and I believe many old-time soda fountains offered them (my grandpa's next venture). U-Bet chocolate syrup was "the syrup of choice" when preparing an egg cream. The man who first produced and bottled it was an acquaintance of Saul's, and he had offered him a "ground floor" partnership, which grandpa turned down. The rest is history; I was told that Saul's acquaintance went on to become a millionaire. Since my mom might never have met my dad had my grandpa taken that opportunity, I am grateful for his decision. Decades later, on the west coast, I came across bottles of U-Bet Syrup in an obscure market in a town I no longer remember. I read the ingredients on the label but purchased the bottle anyway for its nostalgic value. I wondered if the original recipe had artificial flavors and preservatives in it, and whether those additives even existed during the mid-twentieth century. The flavor was different from my memory of it – an example of the adage,

"You can't go home again." The following is my updated version of an old-fashioned favorite.

Mix 1-1/2 Tbsp. each of unsweetened cocoa and honey or maple syrup to a paste in a tall 12 oz. glass. Thoroughly stir in 3/4 cup cold milk until fully blended with the paste. Slowly stir in 3/4 cup cold seltzer until the bubbles reach just above the top of the glass. In my opinion, this drink from my childhood tastes even better when enjoyed through a straw.

Delicious Hot Cocoa

INGREDIENTS
Unsweetened cocoa | 1Tbsp.
Maple syrup | 1-1/2 Tbsp.
Hot milk, 1 or 2% | 1-1/4 cups (or unsweetened non-dairy milk)

DIRECTIONS
In a mug, mix the unsweetened cocoa and maple syrup to a paste. Stir in the hot milk until well blended and a little frothy.

VARIATION
For a mocha, add a 60-40 mix of coffee and hot cocoa, or to your liking.

Pineapple-Nut Quick Bread
Yield: 1 – 8 x 4 or 8-1/2 x 4-1/2 loaf

INGREDIENTS

Whole wheat pastry flour | 2 cups

Sea salt | 1/2 tsp.

Baking soda | 1 tsp.

Nutmeg and cardamom | 1/2 tsp. each

Carrots, grated | 1 cup, packed

Walnuts, chopped small | full 3/4 cup

Extra virgin olive oil | 2 Tbsp.

Juice of fresh lemon | 1 (2 Tbsp.)

Maple syrup | 1/2 cup

Egg, beaten | 1

Pure vanilla extract | 1-1/4 tsp.

Pineapple, crushed in unsweetened
  juice | 1 - 7-8 oz. can

DIRECTIONS

Whisk the dry ingredients together. Stir in the carrots and walnuts. In a separate bowl, whisk together the oil, syrup, lemon, vanilla, and egg. Add to the dry ingredients and stir gently, from the bottom up, until partially mixed. Fold in the pineapple and juice until all ingredients are just blended. Fill your greased loaf pan 2/3 of the way up; make muffins or toasties (p. 45) if you have left-over batter. Bake in a hot 350-degree oven for 50-60 minutes, or until a knife in the center comes out clean and the top springs back to your touch.

Lemon Poppy Seed Muffins
Yield: 12 muffins

INGREDIENTS

Whole wheat pastry flour | 2 cups
Sea salt and baking soda | 1/2 tsp. each
Baking powder | 2 1/2 tsp.
Poppy seeds | 2 Tbsp.
Grated zest and juice from lemons | 2
Juice from additional lemon, kept separate | 1 (2 Tbsp.)
Egg | 1
Buttermilk | 1 cup
Extra virgin olive oil | 1/4 cup
Maple syrup | 1/2 cup
Honey | 2 Tbsp.

DIRECTIONS

In a bowl, combine the poppy seeds with the remaining dry ingredients. Blend the lemon zest and juice with the egg, buttermilk, oil, and syrup in another bowl. Gently stir the wet mixture into the dry ingredients until just combined. Grease muffin tin and fill each cup 3/4 of the way up. Bake in a preheated 400-degree oven for 18-22 minutes, or until a knife comes out clean and the top is springy to the touch. While muffins are baking, warm the honey on the stove until just liquified; stir in remaining lemon juice. When muffins are done, let cool for 10 minutes; transfer to a plate, poke holes in them with a fork, and drizzle with the warm syrup. Sprinkle the tops with the remaining lemon zest.

Apple Crisp
Yield: 1 – 8 or 9" square baking pan

TOPPING INGREDIENTS
Rolled oats and walnuts, chopped together | 1/2 cup each
Whole wheat pastry flour | 3/4 cup
Cinnamon | 3/4 tsp.
Sea salt | 1/4 tsp.
Zest from lemon | 1
Maple syrup | 1/3 cup
Cold butter | 2 Tbsp.

FILLING INGREDIENTS
Unpeeled apples, halved lengthwise, cored, sliced 1/4" | 4-5 cups
Maple syrup | 3 Tbsp.
Lemon juice | 2 tsp.
Apple juice | 1/4 cup
Cinnamon | 1/4 tsp.

DIRECTIONS
Mix the lemon zest and dry topping ingredients in a bowl. With a fork, stir in the syrup to lightly coat. Cut in the butter until it yields pea-size crumbles. In another bowl, toss sliced apples with the next four ingredients. Slide into the greased pan; sprinkle evenly with the topping. Bake in a preheated 360-degree oven for approximately 35 minutes, or until the topping is a deep golden brown and the fruit is cooked through but slightly firm when pierced with a fork. Cover the top with parchment if it starts getting too brown before the apples are cooked. Serve with **Creamy Ginger Sauce**, if desired (see recipe index).

VARIATIONS
For a **gluten-free version**, substitute the whole wheat flour for an equal amount of any combination of corn, oat, buckwheat, or chickpea flour.

For a **vegan version**, with a fork, stir 2 Tbsp. of walnut or olive oil into the flour mix instead of the butter.

Cardamom Pear Ricotta Coffee Cake
Yield: 1 – 8-9" round cake pan

INGREDIENTS
Whole wheat pastry flour | 1-1/2 cups

Baking powder | 2 tsp.

Baking soda | 1/4 tsp.

Sea salt | 1/2 tsp.

Cardamom | 1 tsp.

Eggs, beaten | 3

Small container of ricotta cheese | 8 oz.

Vanilla extract | 1 tsp.

Zest and juice from large lemon | 1

Maple syrup | 1/2 cup

Extra virgin olive oil | 1/4 cup

Bosc pears, unpeeled, 1/2" dice | 3 (approximately 1-1/3 cups)

DIRECTIONS
Mix the dry ingredients in a bowl. Whisk the wet ingredients in another bowl. Gently mix wet into dry until partially blended. Add diced pear and fold until all ingredients are just combined. Spoon into a greased cake pan. Bake in a hot 350-degree oven; check after 30 minutes. A knife inserted in the center should come out clean and the top center should spring back to your touch.

VARIATION
This cake is also delicious with 1-1/3 cups of blueberries in place of the pears.

Maple Walnut Oatmeal Cookies
Yield: 1-1/2 dozen

INGREDIENTS

Whole wheat pastry flour | 1/2 cup

Sea salt | 1/2 tsp.

Baking soda and cinnamon | 1/4 tsp. each

Egg | 1

Milk | 1/4 cup

Maple syrup | 1/2 cup plus 2 Tbsp.

Softened butter and extra virgin olive oil | 2 Tbsp. each

Vanilla extract | 1 tsp.

Rolled oats | 1-1/2 cups

Currants and chopped walnuts, chopped | 1/4 cup each

DIRECTIONS

Mix flour, salt, cinnamon, and baking soda in a bowl. In another bowl, whisk the softened butter with the wet ingredients. Stir into the dry mix, and gently fold in oats, nuts, and currants. Drop by heaping tablespoons onto a greased cookie sheet. Flatten cookies with the back of a spoon. Bake in a preheated 350-degree oven for 10 minutes. Turn baking sheet around, and turn the heat down to 325. Bake another 8–9 minutes, or until nicely browned. Cool on a wire rack before storing.

VARIATION

For **Chocolate Chip Oatmeal Cookies**, chop one 2.8 – 3.5 ounce (approximately 73% cacao content) dark chocolate bar into chocolate chip-sized pieces. Fold them in with the currants and walnuts.

Pecan Pumpkin Quick Bread
Yield: 1 – 9x5 loaf or 12 muffins

INGREDIENTS

Whole wheat pastry flour | 1-1/3 cups

Buckwheat flour | 3/4 cup

Baking powder | 1-1/2 tsp.

Baking soda and Sea salt | 1/2 tsp. each

Cinnamon | 3/4 tsp.

Dried nutmeg, cardamom, and ginger | 1/4 tsp. each

Canned pumpkin or sweet potato | 1–15 oz. can or 1-2/3 cups fresh

Milk | 1/2 cup

Eggs | 2

Extra virgin olive oil | 1 Tbsp.

Grated peel and juice of fresh orange | 1

Maple syrup | 1/3 cup

Pecans (or walnuts), ch. | 1/2 cup

Fresh or frozen unsweetened cranberries (optional) | 1-1/4 cups

DIRECTIONS

Combine dry ingredients in one bowl; whisk wet ingredients in another. Gently stir, folding wet ingredients and the cranberries, if using, into the dry mix until just combined but still slightly lumpy. Bake in a greased loaf pan in a preheated 365-degree oven for 50-55 minutes, or until springy to the touch and a knife inserted in the center comes out clean. For **muffins**, divide evenly in a greased muffin tin, top each with a pecan half; cut baking time to 18-20 minutes.

Blueberry Coffee Cake
Yield: 1 - 8-9" round cake pan

INGREDIENTS

Whole wheat pastry flour | 2 cups
Baking powder | 4 tsp.
Baking soda | 1/2 tsp.
Sea salt | 1/3 tsp.
Buttermilk | 1 cup (or 1/2 cup each of
   low-fat milk and yogurt)

Eggs, beaten | 1
Maple syrup | 1/3 cup
Extra virgin olive oil | 3 Tbsp.
Blueberries | 1-1/2 cups
Walnuts, chopped | 1/4 cup
Cinnamon | 1 Tbsp.

DIRECTIONS

Mix the walnuts and cinnamon in a small bowl; set aside. With a spoon, mix the dry ingredients in a med. large bowl. Whisk the wet ingredients in another bowl until thoroughly mixed, and add to the dry ingredients, stirring from the bottom up, until partially blended. Gently fold in blueberries until all ingredients are just combined. Spoon 1/3 of the batter into the greased cake pan. Sprinkle with half the walnuts and cinnamon. Spoon on remaining batter and top with the remaining nut mixture. Bake in a preheated 350-degree oven for approximately 35 minutes, or until the top springs back to your touch and a knife inserted into the center comes out clean.

VARIATIONS

Partially mash 1 cup of any juicy berry you'd like with 2 Tbsp. of honey. Allow to sit for 20–30 minutes; stir before using. Top each slice of cake with a dollop of plain yogurt and top with the berry mixture. Add a sprig of mint or basil for garnish.
For **Rhubarb Coffee Cake**, substitute 1-1/2 cups of thinly sliced rhubarb for the berries and increase the maple syrup to 1/2 cup.

Lemon Squares

Yield: 1 - 8-9" square baking pan

PASTRY CRUST INGREDIENTS

Whole wheat pastry flour | 1 cup

Sea salt | 1/4 tsp. plus 1/8 tsp.

Cold butter, extra virgin olive oil, and
  maple syrup | 2 tsp. each

Walnuts, finely ground | 1/2 cup

Apple cider vinegar | 1/2 tsp.

Cold water | 2 - 2-1/2 Tbsp.

TOPPING INGREDIENTS

Lemons, finely grated rind and juice | 3
  (1-1/2 Tbsp. rind and 2/3 cup juice)

Lemon, grated rind | 1

Eggs | 3

Maple syrup | 1/2 cup

Baking powder | 1/2 tsp.

Whole wheat pastry flour | 2 Tbsp.

DIRECTIONS

For the crust, grind walnuts in a small food processor or spice mill until they begin to stick together, or chop as finely as you can with a knife and then crush them further with a pestle or potato masher; set them aside. Mix the flour and 1/4 tsp. salt in a medium-sized bowl. Drizzle in 2 tsp. of syrup, the oil, and vinegar while stirring with a fork to combine. Stir in crushed nuts, then cut in butter until it yields pea-sized pieces. Stir in water 1 tablespoon at a time until the dough just holds together when pressed. Press evenly into the bottom of an ungreased baking pan, poke a few holes in the crust with a fork. Bake in a preheated 350-degree oven until lightly browned, approximately 15-18 minutes. Let cool a bit. Meanwhile, for the filling, whisk the eggs, 1/8 tsp. of salt, baking powder, and flour together in a bowl. Whisk in the syrup and 1-1/2 Tbsp. of rind until smooth; stir in lemon juice to combine well. Pour filling into the warm crust, and bake at 350 degrees until just set in the center, approximately 25-30 minutes. The top should feel custardy and springy, not stiff. Allow to cool before cutting in squares. If not serving that day, cool completely before loosely covering, and store in the refrigerator. Before serving, sprinkle with the remaining grated rind.

VARIATION

For a delicious **lemon tart**, substitute an 8-9" tart, springform, or round cake pan, for the square pan. Bake as directed above.

Gingerbread
Yield: 1 – 9x9" baking pan

INGREDIENTS

Whole wheat pastry flour | 2-2/3 cups

Baking soda | 2-1/2 tsp.

Sea salt, ground nutmeg and cloves | 1/2 tsp. each

Cinnamon | 1 tsp.

Ground ginger | 1-1/2 Tbsp.

Eggs, beaten | 2

Maple syrup | 1/4 cup

Molasses | 1 cup

Extra virgin olive oil | 1/3 cup

Applesauce | 2/3 cup

Hot water | 1 cup

DIRECTIONS

Whisk the dry ingredients in a bowl. In another bowl, whisk the sweeteners, eggs, oil, and applesauce until combined well. Add to the dry mix, stirring gently until almost blended. Gently fold in the hot water. Pour into a greased and floured pan. Bake in a preheated 350-degree oven, and check after 35 minutes; the top should spring back to your touch and a knife inserted in the center should come out clean.

VARIATION

Serve with **Creamy Ginger Sauce**: Place 1 cup of plain yogurt in a bowl; lay a paper towel on top of yogurt to soak up excess liquid. Meanwhile, measure and mix together 1 tsp. ground dried ginger (or 2-1/4 Tbsp. minced fresh), 1/8 tsp. cinnamon, a small pinch of salt, 1/2 tsp. each of vanilla and lemon juice, and 2 Tbsp. of honey (slightly warm first if needed for easier blending). Remove paper towel from yogurt; fold in honey and spices until combined.

Banana Bread
Yield: 1 – 9x5" loaf

INGREDIENTS

Whole wheat pastry flour | 1 cup

Oat bran | 2/3 cup

Baking powder | 1 tsp.

Baking soda | 1/4 tsp.

Sea salt | 1/2 tsp.

Egg | 1

Large bananas, overripe | 2 (3/4-1 cup mashed)

Buttermilk | 3/4 cup

Maple syrup | 1/4 cup plus 1 tsp.

Extra virgin olive oil | 3 Tbsp.

Vanilla extract| 1 tsp.

Walnuts, chopped fairly fine |1/3 cup

Cinnamon | 1/2 tsp.

DIRECTIONS

In separate small bowls, mix together the buttermilk and bran, and the cinnamon and walnuts; set aside. Combine remaining dry ingredients in a med. bowl, and add 3/4 of the cinnamon-nut mix. Mash bananas in another bowl. Whisk in remaining wet ingredients; stir in bran mixture. Add the wet to the dry ingredients, and fold gently until just blended. Spoon into a greased pan. Sprinkle the top with remaining nut mixture. Bake in a preheated 350-degree oven for 45-55 minutes, or until the top springs back and a knife in the center comes out clean.

Sour Cream Applesauce Coffee Cake

Yield: 1 – 9" round cake pan

While visiting my aunt and uncle in Connecticut one summer, my Aunt Estelle taught me to make sugar spritz cookies and a delicious Sour Cream Apple Cake prepared with a layer of spiraling cinnamon-coated apple slices in the center of the cake. This is a simplified, less fattening version, but I think of my aunt whenever I bake this tender satisfying cake.

INGREDIENTS

Whole wheat pastry flour | 2 cups

Baking powder | 1 Tbsp.

Sea salt and baking soda | 1/2 tsp. each

Cinnamon and nutmeg| 1/4 tsp. each
   for batter

Cinnamon and nutmeg | 1 tsp. each for
   the spice mix

Cold butter, in eight pieces | 2 Tbsp.

Eggs, beaten | 2

Vanilla extract | 1 tsp.

Maple syrup | 1/2 cup

Extra virgin olive oil | 1 Tbsp.

*Sour cream | 2/3 cup

Unsweetened applesauce | 1/3 cup
   plus 2/3 cup applesauce

DIRECTIONS

Whisk the dry ingredients in a bowl. Cut in the butter to yield pea-sized crumbles. Mix 1/3 cup of applesauce with the remaining wet ingredients in another bowl. Gently mix the wet into the dry until just blended. Spoon 1/3 of the batter into a greased 9" springform or cake pan. Spread the remaining 2/3 cup of applesauce evenly over the batter. Sprinkle with half the spice mix. Tap pan on the counter a couple of times to help applesauce settle. Top with remaining batter and sprinkle with the remaining spice mix. Tap pan again to help top batter settle. Bake in a preheated 350-degree oven for approximately 45 minutes, or until the top springs back to your touch and a knife inserted into the center comes out clean.

*Daisy brand light sour cream, available nationally, is an excellent rich-tasting low-fat sour cream without added chemicals. I highly recommend it for this recipe, or other similar product.

VARIATIONS

Chop a 1/3 cup of walnuts. Add 1/4 cup to the dry ingredients, and the rest to the spice mix.

In place of the 2/3 c. of applesauce for the center of the cake, halve, core, and thinly slice (if the slices are too thick, the cake will dry out before the fruit is cooked) 2-3 Granny Smith, or other baking, apples. Place 1/3 of the cake batter into the greased pan, overlap apple slices in a spiral pattern, gently press down, and sprinkle with half the spice mix (and perhaps a bit more cinnamon). Top with the remaining batter and spice mix. Increase the baking time by 5-8 minutes or until a knife through the center reveals just tender fruit, and the top springs back to your touch. Substitute sliced pear for the apples.

For **Cherry Almond Cake**, omit the 2/3 cup of applesauce for the center of the cake and the 1/4 tsp. each of cinnamon and nutmeg for the batter. Substitute almond extract for the vanilla and add the zest of one lemon. When the wet and dry ingredients are almost combined, fold in 1/3 cup of chopped or sliced almonds and 1-1/2 - 1-2/3 cups of pitted halved cherries. Bake in a preheated 350-degree oven for approximately 45 minutes, or until the top springs back to your touch and a knife inserted into the center comes out clean.

Fudgy Brownies
Yield: 1 – 8-9" square baking pan

INGREDIENTS

Dates, pitted and chopped or torn apart (preferably Medjool) | 1 cup

Water | 2/3 cup

Unsweetened cocoa powder | 3/4 cup

Baking soda | 1/2 tsp.

Sea salt and baking soda | 1/4 tsp. each

Room temperature butter and xv olive oil | 1 Tbsp. each

Vanilla extract | 1 tsp.

Egg | 1

Maple syrup | 1/3 cup plus 1 Tbsp.

Whole wheat flour, all-purpose | 1/3 cup

Walnuts, ch. (optional) | 1/4 – 1/3 cup

DIRECTIONS

Combine water and dates in a saucepan. Bring to a boil, turn off the burner, and remove the pan from the heat. Cool slightly; mash until smooth with a potato masher (use a hand blender or food processor if you have one). Add cocoa, then butter and oil, and continue to mash to form a paste. Stir in salt, baking soda, syrup, and vanilla. Stir in egg until well combined and smooth. Gently fold in the flour until just blended. Spoon into a greased pan, bake in a preheated 350-degree oven for approximately 20-30 minutes, depending on the size and type of pan you use. For fudgy brownies be careful not to overbake. Slightly off-center should spring back to your touch, but the center should feel a little dense and spring back sluggishly. Allow to cool completely. Dip your knife or spatula into hot water for several seconds (and lightly dry) to cut the brownies more easily. Repeat, as needed.

CHAPTER 7

Long-Term Visions Over Short-Term Realities: Assessing Organic and Genetically Engineered Food

Should we ask whether organic food is healthier for us than conventionally grown food, and, if so, is it worth the extra cost for the extra nutrients? When we instead give priority to the long-term picture, that question becomes, "Since we have the technology, along with many examples of successfully run small-, medium- and large-scale organic food businesses, why would we accept production of food by any other means? Why would we endorse the use of poisons that contaminate our soil, water, crops, animals, and the people who handle the toxins if we don't have to?"

At twenty-four I became pregnant with my first (and only) child. I expected that my mom's reaction to the news would include a lecture on my irresponsibility since my soon-to-be husband and I were broke at the time. Instead, she was overjoyed at the prospect of finally becoming a grandma. When I told her how I thought she would react, she simply said, "If people waited until they could afford to have children, not many babies would ever be born." Today I think of this advice more generally in relation to where we spend our money: if we wait until we can afford to buy organic, humanely raised or grown food, then most of us might be eating tainted food forever.

One reason why I think so many people I've spoken to over the years have seemed indifferent to or halfhearted about switching to organically grown food involves their perception that commercial growers spray their fields like individuals might spray their home garden, using small applications of maybe not such bad stuff. But the truth reveals persistent toxic chemical-cocktail applications on many large-, and even some smaller-scale farms and orchards, represent the norm. In a report on chemical use in agriculture on the pubs.usgs.gov website, The U.S. Geological Survey acknowledges, "Ag chemicals (herbicides, insecticides, and fertilizers) are used extensively in the U.S. to increase yields of agricultural crops. Many agricultural chemicals are potentially water soluble and can leach to groundwater or run off to surface water...[which] has been documented in many recent reports."

As consumers, we have the power to pressure the major supermarket chains we support to provide more organic and humanely raised foods. When I shopped for affordable food as a single, struggling mom, those options hardly existed. Fortunately that no longer holds true; shoppers possess more alternatives every day, and, as more and more producers grow organically and competition increases, prices will go down further. We, the consumers, have led that movement. Other consumer-driven efforts include local farmers' markets, and CSAs (Community Supported Agriculture), which can sometimes offer consumers more convenient and affordable options.

Why does organic food typically cost more, especially since organic farmers don't have the expense of purchasing the chemicals used in conventional farming? Two answers come readily to mind. First, chemicals cost far less than labor, and organic farming remains more labor-intensive than conventional farming. Second, organic farmers have to comply with many restrictions mandated by the USDA that lead to higher production costs. According to an article on the Fox News website by The Daily Meal, several other factors help explain the disparity in cost between organic and non-organic foods. Organic fertilizers (like compost and manure) cost more than conventional fertilizers. Crop rotation, including the use of cover crops to build and sustain nutrient-rich soil, represents an additional expense. Organic produce and meats must be kept separate from raw conventional foods, and because organic volumes are substantially lower than non-organic, their shipping costs remain correspondingly higher. Organic certification is expensive, as is the cost to cover the higher losses that result from products with shorter storage and shelf lives because chemical preservatives and ionizing radiation cannot be employed. Securing enhanced living conditions for organic livestock raises additional costs since they must maintain their health without the use of antibiotics. Farmers can spend double the cost for organic compared to conventional feed; further, organic food often grows more slowly than conventional food since no hormones or other synthetic chemicals can be used to stimulate growth. Finally, not only does demand currently overwhelm supply, but higher prices also result from the very expectation that organic food and ingredients will cost more. This only exacerbates and normalizes the high prices, and it will likely remain so until that expectation changes.

Yet even with the additional time and costs involved in producing clean food for the public, farming subsidies to organic farmers represent merely a fraction of the billions that flow each year to conventional commodity growers and automated agri-businesses. Moreover, hidden costs raise the price of purchasing conventional, mass-produced foods. We may pay less at the market, but more and more of our tax dollars go towards cleaning up the toxins left by conventional agriculture, and the increased health care costs generated by them. Professor Jules Pretty, professor of Environment and Society at Essex University, has studied the hidden costs of intensive farming for many years: "The consumer pays three times when they buy intensively farmed food. Firstly, they pay at the shop till. Next, they pay for the same food through their taxes, as modern farming is subsidized through the tax system. Thirdly, the consumer pays again to clean up the damage to the environment caused during the growing and the raising of the food."

If we want the price of organic food to fall substantially, we'll need to transform our current infrastructure. An enormous undertaking, this will require a detailed and coherent plan that will consider everything from rebuilding topsoil on distressed land to providing farmers and their workforce with a clear understanding of just what such changes will require of them. Many farmers will need assistance for the initial cost of conversion, and compensation for the disruption to their yields while switching over to a new system. Further, although most case studies show lower productivity in organic farming over conventional farming, long-term studies, as stated in the scientific journal, *Agriculture, Ecosystem & Environment,* reveal that the yield gap narrows as soil health improves with time. "This is likely due to the time required to fundamentally alter soil properties." Farmers will need to be shielded to some degree from this reality for a specified amount of time. During this period consumers will need protection from price spikes for fresh, frozen, and canned produce, meats, and dairy. Such a radical restoration of our agricultural system will be disruptive, but it will ensure that our tax dollars will benefit all of us. We already possess the technology to convert all of our agricultural land and operations to organic farming. As we put more innovations and "old-fashioned" practices into action, incorporate principles from permaculture, bio-dynamic, and other sustainable systems, and work with economies of scale that protect the land and encourage family farmers and cooperatives, then production, processing, marketing, and distribution costs will all fall. As a result, and with less need to subsidize the agricultural industry in the future, prices to the consumer will decrease as well. As a species, we domesticated fire and agriculture; we developed language, writing, and music; we put a man on the moon; we possess an amazing capacity for significant undertakings, for creativity, learning, understanding, and action. We can certainly do this.

Our nation currently enjoys a thriving "local food" movement. Although I favor locally-grown foods for reasons of energy conservation, community empowerment, flavor, freshness, and diversity, I hope that one day all local foods will be organic. Starting a dialogue with local farmers and market managers might encourage the cultivation of more organic produce in our urban neighborhoods and adjacent agricultural areas. The "Beyond Pesticides" website presents another approach to creating cleaner communities in its praise of Eldredge Lumber and Hardware in York, Maine for replacing harmful synthetic pesticides and fertilizers with organic compatible products. Eldredge is encouraging consumers to employ alternatives by consciously stocking their shelves with those goods. Owner Scott Eldredge asserts that "You're protecting your environment, you're protecting your family, your children and grandchildren, and your neighbors...and people are just loving it...I couldn't be happier." To help other hardware stores and local garden centers transition to holistic lawn and garden care practices, Beyond Pesticides has designed the *Well-Stocked Hardware Store*, which provides product information and tools necessary to support interested store owners and consumers. This guide complements the *Beyond Pesticides' Model Pesticide Policy and Implementation Plan for Communities*, but it can be used independently.

We need transformational reform before we and our children, indeed all animals and our planet, reap the benefits of sustainable farming practices, one reason to begin the process as soon as possible. Meanwhile, we can do our best to connect with neighbors, community organizations and leaders to speak out for effective change, and perhaps find ways to grow our own organic food when availability and costs are challenging.

Some scientists argue that exposure to low levels of chemical residues isn't harmful to humans and that a person would need to consume unrealistic amounts of each vegetable daily for them to be in danger. Others in the scientific community believe the harm comes from consistent and long-term ingestion of these chemicals and the cumulative effect they have on our bodies. In a collaborative essay on the estsjournal.org website - Boudia, Creager, Frickel, Henry, Jas, Roberts, and Reinhardt - consider research based on the science of chemical exposure; "We interact with residues all the time and chronic exposure to a little poison every day can add up to a lot of poison over the course of a human lifetime or...generations. The geographic dispersion of residues can also make an important difference because a little bit everywhere adds up to a lot."

In a Consumer Reports study on chemical residues found in conventional produce, toxicologist, and director of the Food Safety and Sustainability Center, Urvashi Rangan, explains "Tolerance levels are calculated for individual pesticides, but finding more than one type on fruits and vegetables is the rule not the exception...The effects of these mixtures are untested and unknown." The Environmental Working Group (EWG) is an organization of scientists, researchers, and policymakers. They publish an annual report along with two lists (The Dirty Dozen and The Clean Fifteen) on the amount of pesticide residue found in non-organic fruits and vegetables after a thorough wash. Each is based on data from the Department of Agriculture and the FDA. A 2010 article on the PBS website by Jackie Pou reveals, "The fruits and vegetables on 'The Dirty Dozen' list, when conventionally grown, tested positive for at least 47 different chemicals, with some testing positive for as many as 67." A more recent 2015 article on the Good Housekeeping website, by Dan Shapley, shows between thirty and eighty-six different pesticides detected in each of the top twelve. If you're thinking of using this as an excuse for not eating your vegetables, it won't work. Chemical residues found in livestock and their by-products are also a problem, for the conventional grains they eat, and that we eat, contain a variety of contaminants, as well.

Regardless of the foods we consume, it's important to know what we're feeding our bodies. For that reason, I've included EWG's 2021 Dirty Dozen and Clean Fifteen lists. According to the EWG, eating certain varieties of organic produce can reduce the amount of toxins you consume daily by as much as eighty percent. Too many people, however, don't have that option available to them. As Consumer Reports frames it, "The risks of pesticides is real, but the myriad health benefits of fruits and vegetables are, too." This seeming absurdity should act as a call to work with greater speed to transition to organic agriculture.

The Dirty Dozen

Conventionally grown produce found consistently to have the most pesticide residue in their tissue:

Strawberries, Spinach, Kale (Collard and Mustard Greens), Nectarines, Apples, Grapes, Cherries, Peaches, Pears, Bell and Hot Peppers, Celery, and Tomatoes.

The Clean Fifteen

Foods found consistently to have little or no pesticide residue in their tissue:

Avocados, Sweet Corn*, Pineapples, Onions, Papayas*, Frozen Sweet Peas, Eggplant, Asparagus, Broccoli, Cabbage, Kiwi, Cauliflower, Mushrooms, Mangoes, Honeydew Melon, and Cantaloupes.

Sweet corn grown for human consumption reveals little pesticide residue, but it may be produced from genetically modified seeds, as is the case for much of the papaya grown in Hawaii.

The clean fifteen foods aren't necessarily grown with fewer pesticides, but their tissue simply retains less or none of the toxins used to grow them. Although safe for human consumption, these conventionally grown major food crops have a negative impact on the environment and fieldworkers, both domestically and abroad. I encourage everyone to make the switch and fully support organic foods and humanely raised meats for a fitter body, cleaner planet, and healthier farmworkers and children who live in conventional farming communities.

Proponents of modernized, large-scale, conventional production argue for continued chemical use to feed our increasing population and ensure a steady supply of affordable food. But conventional agriculture isn't sustainable. Conventional farmers use increasing amounts of chemicals to produce the same yields and fight the same pests that have adjusted to our attempts to control them. With the proper support, organically grown food and holistic approaches to ranching can supply similar yields of higher quality food without degrading our natural resources. We have the power to change the rules that now benefit the few over the many.

Besides contacting our congress-people, senators, and local representatives, we can also organize bans on certain products. With concerted efforts through social and other media, we could begin with a call to ban the conventionally raised dirty dozen vegetables, perhaps two or three at a time. We could then call for another consumer ban on all conventional factory-farmed pork, then move on to beef, poultry, and then the next group of dirty vegetables. The Delano grape strike of 1965, a battle dedicated to workers' rights, initiated by Filipino-American grape workers and carried on by Cesar Chavez, Delores Huerta, and the United Farm Workers, represents just one famous example of the power of united citizens to transform agricultural practices for workers. In the current National Veal Boycott led by the Humane Farming Association (HFA), activism, education, and consumer support have successfully reduced annual veal production from 3.4 million to under half a million calves, resulting in significant changes to policy that are helping to put an end to the cruel treatment of factory-farmed veal calves. When I lived in Ferndale, I was occasionally able to get local pasture-raised veal. Although I enjoyed the flavor very much, the texture was not very delicate. I certainly miss the fork-tender veal medallions I ate in the past - tender because when kept in enclosures that restrict their movements, calves produce less collagen, the connective tissue that makes meat tough - but I've happily and gratefully sacrificed that pleasure since recognizing its true cost in animal suffering. Consumers possess considerable financial power and when we refuse to buy products that offend our ethical sensibilities and threaten the health of our families we can transform our agricultural landscape.

∽

In our contemporary food marketplace, one cannot discuss organically raised foods without addressing the question of genetically modified foods. My desire to consider GMO foods took me along a challenging route to find information that didn't portray them as completely harmless, as monstrous inventions of the devil, or as part of a topic too technical for a layperson, like me, to understand.

Although I draw what I think is a fair picture of GMOs in our food supply, I will admit that I have a personal bias on the subject. I've never trusted GMO foods because large ag/chemical companies have long introduced them quietly and aggressively into our food chain. I also have a moral objection to moving a gene from one species into another. This process goes beyond hybridization, which manipulates genes from one variety to another variety within the same species to influence the outcome of the fruit, vegetable, or flower produced. Genetic modification technology occurs in a lab, which results in more accurate and faster results, but takes nature out of the actual process of creation. Scientists extract genes from the DNA of one organism and manipulate them to penetrate the host cells of another organism, incorporating new genetic material into the genome of the host. In the traditional cross-breeding of plants, genetic manipulation uses the natural process of breeding within the same species through the transfer of pollen. Although genetic mutations do occur in the wild, they are exceptions. In lab-induced genetic engineering, genes can be, and are, cross-bred with different species: plant, animal, bacterial, and viral. Perhaps the manipulation of genes between species is harmless, perhaps not, but I'm wary of the long-term consequences that technology can bring, especially when transferred from the lab for use in agriculture. Regardless, everyone should be able to make up their own minds about such practices, and, at the very least, have easily accessible, factual information about the foods they eat, where they come from, and under what conditions they grew.

On the biomed.brown.edu website, Deborah Whitman begins with a list of the considerable benefits of genetic technology: the creation of plants that possess pest and disease resistance, herbicide, temperature, drought, and salinity tolerance, nutritional enhancements to combat global malnutrition, the potential to produce edible vaccinations, and the ability to cleanse heavy metal pollution from contaminated soil and groundwater.

Such important benefits, however, do not allay her fear that genetically engineered plants will crossbreed with wild populations, creating unknown future consequences for these vulnerable populations. Whitman stresses this point, explaining that "crop plants engineered for herbicide tolerance and weeds will cross-breed, resulting in the transfer of the herbicide resistance genes from the crops into the weeds. These 'superweeds' would then be tolerant as well." Her paper continues: "when farmers start growing GM crops, they stop growing the old varieties, which are important sources of diverse genes that give plants other desirable characteristics - as in a resistant trait that would be able to combat a new disease or pest that comes along. As we lose the old varieties, we also lose their useful genes." In addition, Whitman highlights the unintended harm that could result to other organisms when a genetically engineered pesticide indiscriminately kills many species of insect larvae, not only the crop-damaging pests.

Moreover, her article explains the costly and lengthy process that brings genetically modified food to market, which involves more and more patented new plant varieties. These factors could lead to higher seed prices that small farmers, here and abroad (particularly those in third world countries), may not be able to afford, thus further widening the gap between the wealthy and the poor.

The learn.genetics.utah.edu website lists benefits similar to those articulated by Whitman and also addresses specific fears raised by GMO technology, such as the concern that the protein products of introduced genes may be toxic or allergenic to particular individuals. Is it possible that the reason we today see more people suffering from allergic reactions to various foods might be because GMO foods have been part of our diet for over twenty-five years? In an article on the BBC website, Dr. Alexandra Santos writes, "the increase in allergies [which is "higher in industrialized nations"] is not simply the effect of society becoming more aware of them and better at diagnosing them....There is no single explanation...but science has some theories." Among those stated are improved hygiene (which leaves the immune system improperly trained), Vitamin D deficiency, pollution, and several decades of significant dietary changes.

An important research article that addresses the application rather than the technology of GM foods comes from an interview by Hannah Kincaid with retired genetic engineer Thierry Vrain, published in Mother Earth News. Throughout her career in molecular biology, Ms. Vrain attempted to assuage people's fears about genetic engineering. When she retired, however, and began to garden as a hobby, she saw how much damage pesticides and fertilizers visit on soil: "At this point, I started reading scientific research showing a problem with genetic engineering. Rats and mice fed genetically engineered Roundup Ready grain were getting sick. At first I couldn't figure it out. My knowledge of the engineering technology made it clear to me that it should be safe." She came to understand that the problem involved the herbicide that farmers apply to all Roundup Ready crops. The active ingredient in Roundup is glyphosate, a molecule invented and patented in the mid-twentieth century by Stauffer Chemical Company to clean mineral deposits off of industrial pipes and boilers. Not only does the molecule bind to other minerals, leaving them non-reactive, it also kills bacteria and plants, so in 1969 the chemical corporation Monsanto purchased the rights to glyphosate and patented it as an herbicide. By the 1980s, genetic engineers designed crops resistant to glyphosate, which allowed farmers to spray those crops with the herbicide, killing the weeds but not the plants.

Vrain goes on to say, "In recent years, many species of weeds have adapted and become resistant, requiring higher and higher doses of glyphosate to be killed [and the] legal levels allowed by the Environmental Protection Agency and Health Canada have increased significantly in the past few years - presumably to accommodate the new reality...Residue levels that were once considered extreme are now seen as normal." Given that small amounts of "glyphosate will kill almost all bacteria - particularly beneficial bacteria - in the gut of animals," this represents a disturbing development.

An Environmental Working Group report, along with other studies, including a recent collaboration between the University of Washington, University of

CA Berkeley, and the Icahn School of Medicine at Mt. Sinai, has revealed possible links to cancer and other health problems through long-term exposure to low levels of glyphosate. The American Cancer Society has classified it as a probable carcinogen. Yet today, according to Environmental Sciences Europe, a peer-reviewed journal, Roundup Weed and Grass killer is "the most heavily used herbicide in history...with an estimated 19 percent of global use happening in the U.S. alone." At the time of their 2016 study, 18.9 billion pounds of glyphosate had been used globally, nearly 75 percent of that figure sprayed on crops within the last 10 years.

Part of this increase is due to the explosion of GM corn and soybean (and other commodity) crops planted worldwide, and part is due to another agricultural utilization of glyphosate. Vrain talked to Kincaid about this less widely known concern: "The use of glyphosate for chemical drying of non-engineered grain and seed crops has also grown exponentially in the past 15 years. . .Some farmers who grow grains and seeds (such as wheat, oats and other cereals, beans, sunflowers, and hemp) now commonly spray a formulation of glyphosate to kill their crops just before harvest. . .It makes for a much easier harvest of grains and seeds." Although glyphosate isn't the best chemical to use for a drying agent, its ability to kill pre-harvest weeds, as well, makes it an appealing choice. A few years ago, my brother Philip and I met in Colorado Springs to help my eighty-nine-year old mother move to Pensacola, Florida, where our brother, Harold, and his wife, Petra, live. While Philip and I drove mom's car from Colorado to the panhandle of Florida, the three of us entertained one another with various diversions. In one such diversion, I read aloud from this very chapter on organic and GMO foods. Previously, Vrain's brief description of the chemical drying process referred to as desiccation, painted only a vague picture in my mind. But as I read about this process while we drove through the agricultural landscape of Kansas, I looked out the car windows at an "as far as the eye can see" acreage of bright green soybean plants on one side of the road, and a similar acreage of uniformly brown, dying corn plants on the other side, an apparent expanse of technologically induced death at the end of July that made the process of chemical drying much more vivid and dramatic. I kept wondering if the soybeans would soon suffer a similar fate.

For over forty years, North American government regulatory agencies, along with Monsanto, have celebrated glyphosate as an effective and safe herbicide; it has become heavily and widely used. However, during the last decade progress in our understanding of the role of the microbiome in animal physiology has revealed that glyphosate is not harmless as previously thought, for it disrupts the community of bacteria present in our microbiome and the microbiome of all animals that ingest it. The trillions of bacterial cells that live in our intestines play a vital role in the health of most of our organs. In light of recent scientific research, I agree with Vrain's conclusion that we remove glyphosate from our food supply by banning "Roundup Ready" technology and the chemical drying of grain and seed crops.

How can we avoid glyphosate in our current food supply? Since much of our conventional grain, seed, and bean commodities go through the desiccation process, avoiding or limiting those foods and the products made from them, like rolled oats and other oat-based breakfast cereals, is one way. Shunning highly processed foods (including conventional soybean, canola, corn, cottonseed, and sunflower oils), and fast foods, in general, is another way to avoid glyphosate. Unless certified organic, the vast majority of processed and fast foods contain glyphosate and/or genetically modified ingredients. According to a 2015 article in TIME (Health) Magazine, written by D.Johnson and S.O'Connor, over 90% of all corn, soybean, cotton, canola, and sugar beets grown in the U.S. (specific numbers over 90% were confirmed on the USDA website), as well as over two million acres of alfalfa grown for hay and commercial animal feed, and thousands of acres of potatoes, zucchini, and yellow squash plants, derive from genetically modified seed.

Other genetically modified products currently in our marketplace include some of the farm-raised Atlantic salmon on the market, certain varieties of browning-resistant apples, most granulated sugar derived from beets, most molasses, and much of the papayas grown in Hawaii, as well as vitamin supplements and medicines, and many food additives and flavorings, including supposedly "natural flavors." The USDA website states that "95% of animals used for meat and dairy eat GMO crops." This would include poultry used for egg production and non-carnivorous farmed fish that are commonly fed genetically modified corn and soy. GMOs have simply become entrenched in our food supply. Yet growing consumer demand for non-GMO foods has begun to change that trend, as people begin to reject products not satisfactorily tested to protect their health and the safety of our planet before they reach the market.

Supporting organic foods presents another way to avoid glyphosate and genetically modified foods. Foods certified "organic" cannot be sprayed with glyphosate at any stage of their growing, harvesting, or drying, nor can they contain any genetically modified ingredients, including livestock feed used for animal production. Unfortunately, while living in the farming community of Ferndale, a number of my neighbors suggested that the USDA hadn't enough inspectors to determine that certified farmers followed all proper organic practices. I've had mixed experiences with inspectors during my professional career, from the health inspectors who have examined the kitchens I oversaw, to planning and building inspectors; some of these interactions were a pleasure, some a frustrating, expensive, and unsatisfactory nightmare. Still, we must support sufficient funding for a necessary service and encourage the evolution of inspection guidelines that can protect our health without undue complexity.

Currently, organic certification remains fairly costly, both in time (much of it spent on paperwork) and money. Many small local growers and manufacturers struggle to compete with larger companies, and the extra annual outlay of money and time can diminish their profit margins to unsustainable levels. I understand their predicament since Geoff and I opted out of organic certification after our first year of business for those very reasons. Instead, many of those food processors and farmers often promote themselves as pesticide- and herbicide-free. However easy it may be for a business owner to make that, and other, claims, I imagine many, if not most, are truthful in that regard. Trusting your intuition about them, researching their business on your own, and seeking out word-of-mouth recommendations or warnings, can all aid in creating trust between you and the small (and big) businesses you patronize.

I'm not convinced that the only danger in GMO foods resides in the toxins used to grow these crops, but that much, at least, is clear, and it represents an immediate threat to our health. Additionally, many non-food products like household cleaners and air fresheners, laundry detergents and softener sheets, cotton-based feminine hygiene products, skin lotions, soaps, perfumes, and sunscreens also contain GMO ingredients, as well as other potentially unsafe additives. We must take care with the products we breathe in and allow our skin to "eat." Please vote for GMO labeling laws and support organic, non-GMO, and glyphosate-free designated foods and products as best you can. Speak with your local market managers about providing more healthy affordable options. In non-organic (primarily skin-care) items, look for the "EWG Verified" seal on the product labels, which guarantees that Environmental Working Group scientists have deemed them free from harmful chemicals. Also, look for the Detox Project's "Glyphosate Residue Free" food and supplement certification and the "Non GMO Project Verified" stamp on food labels. Although "Non GMO Project" doesn't ensure the absence of glyphosate if used in the growing and harvesting process, and "Glyphosate Residue Free" and "EWG Verified" don't ensure the absence of GMOs, they still represent an important step forward. "Organic" certification means the product, and their feed, contains no pesticides, herbicides (including glyphosate), added hormones, or genetic modifications; in organic meat and dairy products, it guarantees the absence of antibiotics as well. If an animal is very ill and needs an antibiotic, the law requires the farmer to treat the animal and take it off the organic market for a specified period.

One consideration not addressed by Vrain in her interview concerns the pollination of genetically modified seed. Seeds travel by wind, in hay, through birds, insects, and other animals. When I farmed in Ferndale, new plants or weeds would pop up every spring, most of them (like poison nightshade, with its 10,000,000 seeds inside of each of 10,000,000 inedible fruits per plant), unwanted. Because wind pollinates GMO seeds, an organic farmer's field in the vicinity of a

GMO farmer's field remains particularly vulnerable to contamination by genetically modified seed blown in from adjacent lands. Organic farmers bear the brunt of costs for preventative measures to avoid GMO contamination, like planting buffer zones and delaying planting so their crops don't flower at the same time as the neighboring GMO crops. These measures consume time as well as money, do not always guarantee success, and can expose the farmer to legal liability. There have already been many instances of the "adventitious presence" of genetically modified material found in organic crops (although a certain amount is allowed by law). Exposure so far has been minimal, but this poses a serious threat to the organic food industry. While driving cross-country on my own in 2012, the absence of organic produce as I got further away from both coasts, even at farmer's markets, greatly surprised me. I can't help wondering if this absence says less about interest in organic crops, and more about the huge swaths of Roundup Ready corn, soy, and cotton fields that dominate our heartland.

Enogen, a variety of corn used for feed and ethanol production, represents yet another genetically modified crop with a strong presence in the American heartland. While Enogen corn can be transformed into renewable fuel, it is neither sustainable nor practical, for it uses more or less as much energy to produce than the fuel it yields. It also requires, like all corn, large amounts of nitrogen-based fertilizers to stimulate its growth. Genetically modified soybeans represent another commodity grown heavily for fuel and feedstock, with yields for fuel not much better than the energy used to grow and process them. Land taken out of (human) food production to grow soy and corn for fuel and feed has contributed to a rise in consumer food prices. Current research shows that a fast-growing native American perennial prairie grass, called Switchgrass, holds more potential than corn in the production of fuel. According to the bioenergy.ornl.gov website, switchgrass would also free land for food production since it doesn't need prime ground to flourish. This hardy and adaptable plant adds organic matter to the soil instead of depleting it, reaches deep in the soil for water and controls erosion, filters runoff, offers habitat, and provides forage. Upon further research, I found mixed reviews regarding the actual energy input compared to its yield. Scientists are also exploring other plants, such as Jatropha, Camelina, and algae, as alternatives for producing fuel.

Yet we should consider the long-term effects that might result from the mass production of any biofuel crop. How much more of our land and water resources will agri-business claim to grow these fuels? What methods of farming will be employed to grow and harvest them? How high will our food prices rise if we keep expanding land use for fuel-production crops? Will we simply trade current for future problems?

Advantages to producing biofuels certainly exist. Algae, for instance, can grow in non-potable water and remove toxins from wastewater; and the fuel produced is compatible with existing U.S. pipelines, refineries, trucks, cars, and airplanes. However, these biological technologies, and others being tested or already in use, employ genetic engineering to develop strains suitable for high biofuel production.

In a 2012 article on the National Center for Biotechnology Information website (ncbi.nim.nih.gov), authors Wang and Brummer discuss genetic engineering in the breeding of specific crops: "Compared with inbreeding species, they [genetically modified forage, turf, and bio-energy crops] have a high potential to pass their genes to adjacent plants...Transgenic technology has been used to improve forage, turf, and bioenergy crops. Because the technology allows the introduction of foreign genes from unrelated species and the downregulation or upregulation of endogenous genes, it offers the opportunity to introduce novel genetic variation into plant breeding programmes." How will this affect our food supply? We already know that genetically modified organisms cross-pollinate with plants in nature: can organic and bio-dynamic systems co-exist with GMOs, or will the GMOs eventually transform our green spaces? How will widespread planting of genetically modified crops for both fuel and food affect all the wildlife dependent on the earth for their food? Is it possible that GMO plant growth contributes to our declining populations of birds, bees, and butterflies? The same article by Wang and Brummer states that, as of 2010, "The accumulated growth areas from 1996 - 2010 exceeded 1 billion hectares [approx. 2-1/2 billion acres].

The number of countries planting biotech crops reached 29 in 2010 and the top ten countries each grow more than 1 million hectares. The United States remains the biggest adopter of transgenic crops, with 66.8 million hectares planted in 2010, which represent 45% of the global biotech area."

What if we were to manipulate switchgrass and algae (and other crops) without crossing the line into genetic modification? If using more traditional hybridization techniques requires sacrificing greater yields, larger profits, and cheaper costs to consumers, might that difference make production still worth it to us?

Shouldn't we rather put more resources into developing affordable long-range electric vehicles (including medium- and heavy-duty trucks), electric farm equipment and school buses, and clean energy microgrid charging stations? Shouldn't our local transportation planning involve bicycles (including electrically powered bikes), safe walking paths, and coordinated mass transit systems? Couldn't we continue to advance cleaner ways to heat and cool our homes, all while creating a significant number of good-paying jobs in the process? What if we became serious about actually limiting our energy consumption as a nation? Without a concerted effort by consumers to govern our own consumption and waste, there will be little political will for government and business to work expediently together to make necessary changes. After all, they respond primarily to our continuing demand for more and cheaper energy and goods, whatever the source.

Consumers can lead this transformation by curbing our own patterns of consumption, changing personal buying and discarding habits, before asking how our communities could then participate in new modes of production and consumption. If, as a parent, you asked your children to sacrifice the throw-away plastic water bottles and "cute" individually packaged snacks in their lunchbox for reusable bottles and containers, don't you think that most children old enough to understand would embrace the opportunity to avoid excessive waste and help create a cleaner planet? The emergence of Greta Thunberg as an international celebrity, and the environmental youth movement she helped grow, indicates the importance of children and young adults in our efforts to respond to climate change.

In his important work, *Encyclical on Climate Change and Inequality (On Care for Our Common Home)*, Pope Francis writes, "Compulsive consumerism is one example of how the techno-economic paradigm affects individuals. This paradigm leads people to believe that they are free as long as they have the supposed freedom to consume...When people become self-centered and self-enclosed, their greed increases. It becomes almost impossible to accept the limits imposed by reality. In this horizon, a genuine sense of the common good also disappears. As these attitudes become more widespread, social norms are respected only to the extent that they do not clash with personal needs." However, he also goes on to say, "Yet all is not lost. Human beings, while capable of the worst, are also capable of rising above themselves, choosing again what is good, and making a new start, despite their mental and social conditioning."

We could immediately begin many projects that would make an important positive impact on our environment, and we could expand existing projects. Beyond the significant reduction of individual and community consumption and waste, we could more actively advance certification for the sustainably harvested status of several products, including palm oil, soy, cattle, wood, and all biofuels. We continue to destroy vast sections of forests worldwide to produce these commodities that contribute to our fuel and food supplies, homes, and furnishings. As consumers, we can buy recycled goods, demand affordable sustainable commodities, avoid single-use packaging and bags. We could decorate our homes with live greenery and help plant food forests, trees, and perennial herb lawns. We can keep our auto vehicles maintained for optimal fuel efficiency. According to Consumer Reports, replacing our tires, as needed, with all-season low rolling resistance tires "can improve fuel economy by an additional one or two mpg... Moreover, you generally don't have to pay more to get a tire with better rolling resistance." The report adds that keeping our tires properly inflated, checking them at least monthly when the tires are cool, will further improve our gas mileage. Perhaps, we could even cut down on gas-powered travel.

We're also able to conserve on the water we use, and on heating and air-conditioning by sealing our homes from drafts and setting the thermostat one or two degrees higher or lower. We could conserve on laundry loads by using a towel or wearing an article of clothing, unless unsavory, one more time before throwing it in the hamper, and by choosing to purchase less plush towels that dry more quickly. In an article in "Scientific America," David Biello surprisingly relates that, "U.S. citizens spend more money on electricity to power devices when off than when on. Televisions, stereo equipment, computers, battery chargers and a host of gadgets and appliances consume more energy when seemingly switched off, so unplug them instead."

With pressure from constituents, our government could put into play beneficial projects that have been stalled in Congress for years: modernize our national rail and help update regional bus systems; when feasible, offer secure lockers, map kiosks, and bicycle rental areas at rail and bus depots. The government could open electricity markets to competition. We could tax major polluters, including those who emit carbon and methane, as well as those who allow various toxins to leach into our soil and water. The money collected from such taxes could be used to advance carbon farming, an important agricultural practice that reduces greenhouse gas emissions and captures carbon by holding it in vegetation and soil. "Pollutant tax" proceeds could also be used with regulatory support to encourage more renewable energy and regenerative agricultural, forestry, and water projects on Native American tribal lands. This would benefit us all, and present the opportunity of energy independence and clean local food and water sources for our indigenous populations. These projects would give them tools to create revenue, training programs, and well-paying jobs more in line with their deep cultural reverence for our natural world than gambling casinos.

In agricultural communities, our government can further advance precision agriculture, which utilizes technology to increase yields and profitability while decreasing the use of water, land, labor, fertilizers, and pesticides. They could help farmers who want to transition to growing crops and livestock more compatible with changing local climates and available resources; they can help more farmers turn ag waste into fuel and other "value-added" products that would both improve the environment and farm incomes.

We could call for comprehensive tax incentives for building homes and offices using primarily non-toxic materials. We could exercise our purchasing power to promote the transition from our current Linear Economy, which transforms natural resources into manufactured products that become waste, to a Circular Economy, which the EPA defines as an economy that "reduces material use, redesigns materials to be less resource-intensive, and recaptures "waste" as a resource to manufacture new materials and products." Governments and businesses globally are transitioning towards this economic model; and although our government is moving forward with programs that are leading us in that direction, they often progress slowly because of bureaucratic inefficiencies, media indifference, and a shortfall of political and constituent will.

We could work with speed to integrate ancestral knowledge, traditional fire management techniques, and current wildfire strategies and advance other measures that would lead to better-managed forests and protections for the nation's big trees. We can enforce our "no littering" laws for individuals and businesses, and levy much harsher penalties on industries that continue to dump toxic waste into our waterways. The fines collected could help fund existing conservation projects nationwide that urgently need additional resources.

Coordinated strategies for disposing of our waste more responsibly could be created. Why are certain localities and states better at recycling than others? Are some of us currently wasting precious water and time washing recyclables only to have much of them end up in landfills? Local and state leaders could emulate successful systems from here and abroad. They could partner with each other, with waste management agencies, packaging manufacturers, recycling businesses, and composting companies, to organize a cohesive system that employs the most efficient and convenient ways to recycle, privileging a transparency that allows consumers to see just where their recyclables end up.

To help reduce the number of plastic water bottles, and afford clean drinking water to more people, our counties can direct the installation of modern, filtered water fountains in all schools and many public spaces (perhaps modeled after France's successful system, Eau de Paris). Internationally, governments could further work together with industry to advance green hydrogen generation and electric mass transit vehicles, including medium-range airplanes and ships. They can also end the present-day practice of airline tankering, carrying more fuel than necessary for a flight. This practice saves money when the price of gas is lower at the airplane's starting point than at its destination. Yet this tactic adds weight to the craft, increasing fuel consumption and thus the amount of CO_2 emitted. Similarly, governments can impose a reasonable speed limit on cargo ships to curb their fuel consumption. They could help safeguard mangrove forests and coral reefs, and pass the Global Ocean Treaty. They can also make changes to import and export tariffs and taxes that would reduce costs on sustainably-produced merchandise and correspondingly increase costs on the luxury goods, and ultimately all goods, whose production or extraction damages our already fragile ecosystems.

There already exist exciting and successful environmental projects all around our globe. Many countries, often with the help of conservation organizations, now protect their wetlands, build climate-friendly infrastructure, and have committed to mass tree planting projects. China has taken the lead in creating "sponge cities," urban environments engineered to capture and re-use rainwater to recharge aquifers, irrigate urban farms, gardens, and tree-lined walkways. Many green rooftops have been installed, and concrete pavements replaced with wetlands. The Netherlands has instituted a dynamic "Room for the River" program, building more efficient flood protections while working closely with local communities to create more sustainable urban spaces. They've also installed outdoor red LED lighting and other specific LED lights that are not so disruptive to nocturnal wildlife and save on energy as well. Canada has committed itself to a variety of wetland, wastewater, and clean water projects. Communities in Africa and in other semi-arid and dryland environments are building "sand dams," low-cost structures used for harvesting and conserving rainwater.

Myriad "green" projects now save energy and water resources in every country, including our own, like "Green Streets" in Portland, Oregon, where the integration of multi-use transportation systems, healthy watersheds, and parks create more resilient neighborhoods. L.A.'s "Greenstreet" on Elmer Ave. utilizes ditches filled with native plants, bioswales, and permeable sidewalks to divert storm water, allowing it to be absorbed by the soil and filter into underground aquifers. Los Angeles has also installed off-the-grid solar streetlights, using long-lasting LED lighting. Chicago now has over 500 Green Roofs within its city limits. A green roof is described on the National Park Service website as "a layer of vegetation planted over a waterproofing system that is installed on top of a flat or slightly-sloped roof." Included on the NPS list of benefits gained from green roof installations are: improved stormwater management, improved air quality, reduced energy costs, improved building insulation, cooler rooftop air temperatures that enhance the efficiency of rooftop HVAC equipment, reduction in "urban heat island effect," increased urban green spaces, and extended roof life. Cities and towns of all sizes are restoring their creeks and riverbeds, improving water quality and stormwater capture and drainage, creating scenic trail systems, and preserving native landscapes.

Although our country can do much on its own, we still need to work with other nations and agree to meet our worldwide commitments, for the Paris Climate Accord represents the most efficient way to address problems we share with everyone on the planet. In his Encyclical on Climate Change, Pope Francis stresses that "Halfway measures simply delay the inevitable...the issue cannot be addressed piecemeal...We need to see that what is at stake is our own dignity. Leaving an inhabitable planet to future generations is, first and foremost, up to us."

Solar, wind, and micro-wind farms, clean modernized waste-to-energy plants, along with other renewable alternatives, can speed our progress to a green future when placed in locations that are responsibly and ethically thought out. They can't always be located in someone else's backyard, but we can endeavor to have them built as aesthetically pleasing as possible. We must support and invest wisely in a diversified mix of renewable energy sources to achieve a cleaner planet. Unfortunately, no perfect solutions exist. Large-scale wind generation is disruptive to surrounding ecosystems and fatal to many birds. More appropriate site selection that considers migratory paths and breeding grounds, pooled GPS data on the flight behavior of birds when near wind farms, and ongoing research to further mitigate impacts on habitat and human communities have helped, but we need to do more. Solar technology and electric vehicles are reliant on the mining of minerals for the batteries they require. Considerable resources are being invested to improve battery technology, with mixed results. In a promising article on the CleanTechnica website, physicist and energy analyst, Amory Lovins, details how improved batteries store more energy per kilogram, are longer-lasting, and are being recycled more efficiently and "reincarnated" (successive uses of the same materials). Novel battery chemistries are also being developed that don't require rare earth minerals. Hopefully, these innovations will continue to improve. However, it's true that everything we do, especially on an industrialized scale, affects our planet. To protect the earth and her inhabitants, we must avoid "solutions" that may have irreversible ecological consequences that can't be undone and replaced with better alternatives as our technology and understanding improves, thus my caution regarding biofuel production in its present form. At the same time, we must consider less than ideal strategies as we make the transition from our current to a green technology. Steve Clemmer, director of the Union of Concerned Scientists, for instance, recommends that we "keep safely operating nuclear plants running until they can be replaced by other low-carbon technologies. This would also give time for plant owners to develop worker and community transition plans to prepare for their facilities' eventual retirement and decommissioning." Indeed, workers and communities affected throughout our transition to a clean economy will need protection; securing their welfare, here, and globally, is key to any plan's ultimate success.

We have the know-how and the technology to produce our food and energy sustainably, and harnessing energy from renewable sources like the sun and wind is available to all countries. It's not hard to imagine the beneficial impact clean energy independence would have on the earth and its populace. Symphonizing these goals would be an efficient way to achieve both. In an interview with Walter Isaacson on Amanpour and Company, economic and energy expert, Daniel

Yergin relates, "about 70 percent of the costs of food actually is energy, from synthetic fertilizer and tractors, from trucks to move it...."

Effective trials already in place in this country combine solar power and agriculture in ways that produce both food and energy on the same land. This provides additional income and cheaper power to farmers, compensating them for lower yields. Farmers can now install solar panels with minimal soil disruption: this new generation of panels no longer requires concrete footings and can be installed in ways that allow sunlight to reach crops and heavy equipment to pass through. Technological advances will soon produce for the mass-market translucent panels that allow even more sunlight to reach crops, and bi-facial panels that can catch reflected sunlight from both sides. Subsidies currently going to farmers to grow Enogen corn and soy-based biodiesel would be much better spent on efforts that combine organic farming and renewable energy production, possibly on some of the very farms now growing genetically modified corn and soybeans.

Solar can not only integrate well with our current power systems but can also work as a stand-alone microgrid. This particularly appeals to me as a northern Californian recently affected by extended power shut-offs due to large fires south and east of us. Apparently, such shutdowns will become the new norm as utility companies and firefighters grapple with the massive fires that now threaten my state. Indeed, the coronavirus crisis has dramatized the need throughout our country for small communities and individual counties to become as self-reliant as possible. The switch to solar can at the least forward the goal of energy sustainability, and often quite seamlessly. New solar systems can be installed in the large outdoor parking lots found at hospitals, big box stores, airports, colleges, and stadiums everywhere, vehicles benefiting as well from the shelter they provide. Solar panels can also become part of decorative exterior walls, installed as well on rooftops of existing buildings without monopolizing more land for energy production. The added independent storage and distribution of power that such projects can create means that many areas will be able to retain power even if the main grid goes down. This infrastructure would also serve our national security interests as modern-day cyber-warfare becomes more prevalent.

What solutions do you support that would help make your neighborhood cleaner, healthier, and more resilient? Perhaps local town halls, VFW posts, granges, community centers, and schools can host weekly or monthly "pop-up" or "pot luck" Neighborhood Cafés that attempt to address these challenges. Many of the suggestions I make throughout this book are offered in what I call a "Neighborhood Café" style. Some are already in the works and can be strengthened with additional attention and support; others are meant to be worked on further, based on real-life complexities. Getting our common sense thoughts down in written form is a start, and with helpful input from others, they may develop from there. Dedicated to solutions, common ground, and a vision of what individuals want to see in their communities, Neighborhood Cafés could help integrate those ideas, and local government officials and business leaders can be invited to community dialogues that could lead to eventual change.

Such change will depend on the research that has for centuries governed the development of agriculture in this country, and we might want to re-evaluate where the bulk of our money goes towards that purpose. Today, the Chamber of Commerce, the U.S. Farm Bureau, the fossil fuel industry, insurance and banking institutions, and the industrial food, drug, and chemical companies, are all interconnected. Too often their powerful lobbying groups work cooperatively to entrench the status quo and cast doubt on climate science. In a "60 Minutes" program featured on the CBS News website, Mike Wallace reveals that, while tens of thousands of annual dues-paying farmers are sinking into debt, the Farm Bureau, a non-profit, tax-exempt organization, "has been building a for-profit business empire worth billions. And they are investing millions of dollars in some of the same giant agribusiness corporations the Farm Bureau's members say are driving them out of business...[and in] many for-profit interests outside of traditional farming. Many, if not most, of the Farm Bureau's members are not farmers at all and live in urban areas far from rural America." On Nebraska's PBS and NPR Stations website, Peggy Lowe from Harvest Public Media reports that the massively-funded Farm Bill that sets U.S. ag policy "is no longer the purview solely of agricultural interests...Farm Bill lobbying is a reflection of big business." She goes on to cite some of the biggest contributors to the 2018 farm bill, which include the U.S. Chamber of Commerce, Exxon, DuPont, and Monsanto (now part of Bayer). The farm bill was first created to help stressed farmers during the depression. Now it's being directed by "Fortune 500 leaders in banking, trade, transportation and energy to non-profits worried about food stamps and global hunger."

Lowe also notes, "The American Bankers Association [as] one of the groups that will benefit most from the bill thanks to a shift away from the safety net policy of direct subsidies to crop insurance." On the National Sustainable Agriculture Coalition website, Craig Schmitt, an organic grain farmer in Montana, states, "Crop insurance rules get in the way of developing a resilient system in the face of growing extreme weather and climate disruption." The NSAC confirms that those rules, which define what can be insured, have "tended to reinforce current agriculture practices that are significantly climate-unfriendly..." This seems a good illustration of the heavy investment the banking industry still has in the fossil fuel and chem/ag industries. Through decades of research, we've recognized and developed systems that enable us to better use and work with our natural resources. These achievements could still stave off and reverse some of the worst effects of our changing climate. Big business obstruction keeps us from putting into practice things we already know how to do, clearly showing the powerful interconnection, destructive influence, and the hold, unchecked lobbying and our current campaign financing laws have over our country.

Much of our tax revenue that currently supports research grants goes to chem/ag, and drug companies, rather than supporting independent researchers who have no conflicts of interest regarding their work. Even our most trusted resources - the local agricultural extension services and land-grant university system – should today be regarded with a more questioning eye. The federal government established land-grant universities in 1862 when it deeded tracts of land to every state to promote research for the development of better seeds, as well as new plant varieties for farmers who could benefit from such research with increased productivity, improved livelihoods, and safer products. These advances depended on public investment from state and federal governments.

The sharing of knowledge and scientific advances between universities and farmers occurs primarily through the USDA extension offices situated throughout the country. Geoff and I frequently visited our local field office in Eureka, benefiting from their expertise and advanced research. For the most part, I view the expert staff and services offered by the extension system as an important asset to our country, its farmers, and gardeners. However, in the 1980s, federal policies began encouraging land-grant colleges to partner with the private sector on agricultural research. In recent decades, government funding has slowed and agribusiness has filled the gap. A report published by Food and Water Watch (*Public Research, Private Gain*) details many specific examples of land-grant schools that have become dependent on industry "to underwrite grants, endow faculty chairs, sponsor departments and finance the construction of new buildings." Industry funding arrangements can, and too often do, legally restrict or eliminate specific research, the publication of certain results, and the open disclosure of funding sources without the approval of the corporate patent holder. Key aspects of genetically modified crops, like ongoing yields, soil conservation, and food safety, remain to a great extent unstudied.

Even the federal government's USDA funding supports these compromised research agendas, reflected through our National Farm Bill, which directs our tax dollars to "prioritize research for commodity crops like corn and soybeans, which are the building blocks of processed foods and the key ingredients in factory-farmed livestock feed." The USDA prioritizes crops that produce bulk oils and sugars, key ingredients in processed foods. This misguided funding continues even as our population grapples with significant increases in diet-related illnesses, obesity, and diabetes.

Affordable access to a healthy food supply will benefit us all. If you agree, let your local, state, and federal representatives know how you feel. Regarding our health and safety, let us demand a farm bill that safeguards our well-being and our land, and insist that impartial parties perform a considerable amount of the needed research towards those goals. This would take much of the work and sphere of influence out of the hands of food, drug, and chemical companies (and those influenced by them) that stand to gain or lose billions of dollars on the outcomes.

Research and development play a key role in determining our lives and the direction of our society, particularly in medicine and agriculture. Technology is generally essential to its application. This has resulted in many positive changes, including those in energy and water conservation, and other efficiencies, as well as helping to build an infrastructure that can harness the power of renewable energies. However, technology advances so quickly that at times it seems impossible for us to respond both intellectually and ethically. Yet the moral questions raised by technological transformation demand answers as quickly as possible; many of those involve our food supply.

A new technology that genetically modifies crops within their own species through gene editing provides one important example of the complex ethical questions raised by science in the contemporary world. This technology has allowed scientists to save the Cavendish banana and cacao by making them disease-resistant. We're also creating drought-tolerant soybeans, high-yield tomatoes and rice, and larger, hardier sweet potatoes with increased beta carotene to improve food security in Africa, caffeine-free coffee, flavor-enhanced strawberries, high-fiber wheat, soy oil that possesses a fat profile close to that of olive oil, and non-browning apples and mushrooms. Promising work might also create a heat- and disease-resistant avocado by modifying the tree's rootstock rather than the fruit-bearing scions. Do all of these possibilities sound attractive to you? Do any of these possibilities sound alarming?

These products are currently being developed for the market since no FDA restrictions govern the development of new technologies that appear safe. This gene editing technology works on animals, as well. According to an article by Rowan Jacobsen in Eating Well Magazine, "Researchers have big plans for hornless cows (which wouldn't have to undergo painful and labor-intensive dehorning), chickens that are immune to bird flu, and pigs that don't get porcine respiratory syndrome." Do these possibilities seem attractive?

As potentially exciting as such developments might sound, it concerns me that in many cases we forsake proven realities, sound methods, and traditional ideas for new technologies that may exacerbate problems created by our consumption economy and global pollution. I strongly support science, but not always its careless application. We already possess a chemical-free "swiss-water" process that removes most of the caffeine from coffee; there already exist many older varieties of strawberries, bananas, and avocados that taste delicious and grow in a variety of climates; bulgur and other whole grains already contain a high-fiber content, while existing varieties of apples and mushrooms brown slowly. When we look at products as merely commodities, we fail to recognize the abundant diversity in nature's pallet. Technology seems morally lost to me when it disregards existing remedies because they're not technical enough, when it fails to acknowledge the connection between environmental and human health. No matter how much we tinker with our food supply, strong bodies and immune systems cannot exist for long in unhealthy environments unless, perhaps, you're a rat or a cockroach.

Can we co-exist with same-species genetic modification technology? The FDA now deems it safe, but might we eventually suffer negative consequences from its uncontrolled proliferation? How will its cross-breeding in nature affect our natural world in the long-term? How will our consumption of gene edited foods and medicines affect our long-term health, if at all?

The FDA currently regulates gene editing in animals, and for now, it remains too costly for the mass market. But it won't likely stay that way for long - and what comes next? Scientists already contemplate gene editing in human subjects. One procedure, somatic gene therapy, focuses on modifying genes to cure diseases in living subjects; these modifications would not be transmitted to the next generation. But in a second procedure, germline engineering, they would, for these modifications are designed to "improve" the human species, not only eliminating genetic diseases, but allowing scientists to engineer higher intelligence, superior physical attributes, and even specific personality traits. Germline engineering does not address an existing person's health needs, but instead modifies reproductive cells, affecting the offspring and all descendants.

He Jiankui, a Chinese biophysics researcher, was fined and sentenced to three years in prison for gene editing the embryos of twin girls in 2018; he attempted to make them HIV resistant. Subsequently, the World Health Organization launched a global registry to track research on human genome editing, trying to halt any CRISPR (a gene editing tool) experiments and other work that might lead to the birth of altered humans.

Many scientists want to delay the progress of this technology while society as a whole, rather than just the scientific community, considers its ethical dimension, but many do not; the scientific community remains split on this issue. Much of the technology already exists, although further research and testing are necessary before it can be brought to the mass market. Its chief virtue lies in its potential to eradicate the many genetic diseases, conditions, and defects that cause so much human suffering. But we do not yet possess any clear understanding of the risks involving unintentional edits and long-term persistent editing, which might generate unforeseen biological consequences. Many opponents argue that the use of somatic gene therapy and embryo screening could accomplish similar disease reduction more safely and ethically. A further argument against germline editing corresponds to that concerning genetically modified crops: as we commit to modifying genes for preferred traits the gene pool eventually diminishes, both in plants and potentially in humans as well.

If the FDA declares germline engineering safe, and it becomes available to the wider public, who will first gain access to this technology? Will it be people who have the money to pay for it? Will that widen the gap further between the haves and the have nots? Will all parents not feel the need to use this technology so that their children won't get left behind? In a National Geographic article on the pros and cons of germline engineering, Marcy Darnovsky cautions, "Permitting human germline gene editing for any reason would likely lead to its escape from regulatory limits, to its adoption for enhancement purposes, and to the emergence of a market-based eugenics that would exacerbate already existing discrimination, inequality, and conflict. We need not and should not risk these outcomes."

Since the invention of the atomic bomb over a half-century ago, we have succeeded in not annihilating the human race. We've achieved this without a "restraint" gene implant, utilizing instead our capacity to choose not to cross certain lines, even though we can. The key to human evolution lies in our spiritual development and ability to use our intelligence wisely. Embracing the evolution of our individual and collective lives determines both the quality of life and the fulfillment of our continuing search for meaning and happiness. That search has nothing to do with our personal appearance, competitive advantages, acquisition of possessions, or stubborn embrace of the fleeting illusions of society. Collective character alone endures, determined through our progeny and those we touch during our lifetime.

My mom taught her three children to value kindness and balance in our lives, while my dad brought us up emphasizing two recurring themes: "The true value of a person doesn't lie in a prestigious, well-paying job, but in all the ways they leave the world a better place. It doesn't matter if you dig ditches for a living or choose to do something else, do it as wholeheartedly and as well as you can"; "[almost] everything in moderation is O.K." I didn't always follow my parents' advice, but I took their lessons to heart and they still serve me well, particularly when I contemplate the fruits of our technological society. Can we control the consequences of technological change? What effect is technology having on the levels of happiness and stress in our lives, and in our children's lives? What defines the purpose of social media, genetic engineering, nanotechnology, artificial intelligence, and robotics? Will such technologies allow for well-planned improvements to the health and well-being of people and the planet, or will they transform people, society, and the planet beyond recognition? Will our future accomplishments hold any meaning if achieved through genetic enhancements? Scientists are in the business of discovery, but are they compelled to make any and every discovery? Are technicians driven to develop any algorithm and their subsequent "tweaks"? Are tech-leaders addicted to the authority they derive from overseeing the collection of personal data and the distribution of information? And are we, as consumers, so addicted to the acquisition of the next gadget, convenience, and upgrade that we cannot stop this momentum? Can we imagine an alternate vision of what the future might hold for us? I'm not the only one who thinks we're capable of improving and advancing our species without genetic enhancements and other manipulations. I know we can make agricultural and medical advances without using germline engineering; we already are.

Why not put more of our resources into the root causes of disease, like stress, diet, and pollution, before we start permanently altering the genes in humans, other animals, and plants? Let us further intertwine eastern and western medical philosophies and practices, joining clean technology to holistic agriculture for optimal health. Let us direct the trajectory of science and technology, using restraint and common sense to determine how we want them to work for us and future generations. We need to have many conversations before genetic modification, germline engineering, and other irreversible technologies become an integral part of how our society and species evolve. Perhaps a Neighborhood Café can provide a warm, inviting place to begin such a dialogue, as we develop a blueprint for a wiser, more self-reflective, and inclusive evolution of man/womankind.

In chapter two, I list organizations dedicated to raising plants that are pest, herbicide, disease, temperature, drought, and salinity tolerant, that bear nutritionally enhanced produce, and that can help clean heavily toxic soil and groundwater without using GMO technology.

For gardeners, there are several seed companies that only sell non-GMO seeds; many of them specialize in organic seeds and the preservation of older varieties through open-pollination, and some sell seeds in bulk for farmers. More can be found online, but I've listed a few here: Fedco Seeds Cooperative, Seed Savers Exchange, Redwood Organic Seeds, Southern Exposure Seed Exchange, Territorial Seed Company, Uprising Seeds, True Leaf Market, Adaptive Seeds, Trees of Antiquity, and primarily for commercial producers, Vitalis Organic Seeds.

CHAPTER 8

Assessing Factory Food; Recipes

Ultimately, we cannot fully clean our food supply without changing how we treat animals on factory farms, the source of most of the meat on our tables. I don't think we will ever quite realize our physical, mental, and spiritual health as long as we treat immorally the animals we consume. Many organizations - some listed in chapter two - dedicate themselves to the health and well-being of the animals that are raised to serve as our food supply, and to the dignity of the laborers who work with them. The more people who support their work, who talk to their government representatives, who ask their local grocers to offer more humanely-raised meats, and who purchase those meats, the more quickly competition and infrastructure will increase, while prices will fall.

Supporting local, ethically organized, small- and medium-sized family farms can help us make the transition to a more appropriate caretaking of land, animals, and workers. We can pressure our representatives to include in the Farm Bill the re-appropriation of funds to support more cooperatives and local processing plants. These facilities can serve not only to slaughter and package (or oversee sanitary mobile butchering services), but to act as joint storage, marketing, and distribution points within a shared shipping network of small and mid-sized local farms. A similar storage, distribution, wholesale and retail marketing infrastructure could work for smaller produce, dairy, and egg farmers, as well. These networks would bring down costs for farmers who struggle to compete with factory and other large farms, and consumers who currently find it too financially burdensome to support organic production and more humane conditions on farms. Farms within the network could receive funding for implementing sensible guidelines for more fair and regenerative agricultural practices. Furthermore, we could design these processing plants to produce the energy needed for their operations through a combination of solar panels, mini wind turbines, and local agricultural waste. These networks could help protect small and mid-size farms and generate much-needed county and state taxes, creating local jobs and cleaner communities in the process. Giving farmers the tools to process and store their products, and sell their goods directly to the market or consumer if they choose, is vital in their ability to diversify and profit more from their labor.

Today's farmers are being squeezed in all directions by agribusiness, government, and the consumer. Corporate agribusiness builds its wealth by selling the tools of the farmer's trade, like seeds, feed, fertilizers, and equipment. Major processors buy what the farmer produces for the lowest price possible; then they process it and sell it profitably. When animals are the commodity, processors may fatten them up first (in lots or confined finishing operations) to increase their value before they process and sell them. Industrial in nature, they can most often bring the finished products to the consumer for less money, and earn a greater profit, than can an individual farmer. The customer reinforces this cycle in his or her search for the lowest prices. Local cooperatives could offer farmers more bargaining power and perhaps more options to produce what, and sell to whom, they want; they could help protect the consumer, as well.

Walmart and Costco now participate in the business of agriculture. Walmart has not only its own Angus beef and dairy herds, but processing plants as well. Costco is raising and processing many of the chickens it sells. Some farmers benefit from the contracts they enter into with these mega-companies, but many conventional and organic farmers are left scrambling to find new buyers for their products, or they end up displaced. Nebraska is the state hosting Costco's new chicken raising venture. Jim Hansen, president of the Nebraska Farmers Union is watching this development, not sure how it will play out in the end. For an article on the Farm and Dairy website, reporter Alan Guebert spoke to him about big retailers getting involved in agriculture. Hansen describes them as having ultimate control of production, quality, costs, distribution, and profit. He warns, "I have said that farmers who sign these contracts are volunteering to get run over by a bus because total integration means the total elimination of markets...[they] become the only market."

One example of that in play was related to me by Jim Regli, a generational dairy farmer in Ferndale, and part of the Organic Valley cooperative. Expressing his concern, he explained, "when companies like Organic Valley negotiate with Walmart or Costco, they are beaten down so much, they actually lose money in order to gain contracts." He emphasizes the need for consumer-driven change in the marketplace.

There was a time when Geoff and I considered taking our local food company national. After researching that prospect we decided against it. Meeting the demands of the "big" markets we would need to enter, and those of the distributors we would need to represent our products, made the likelihood of success as a small family operation improbable. Keeping our prices competitive in just our supportive local area was a great enough challenge.

Large companies purchase their ingredients, or finished products, in greater quantities than small businesses, and therefore they enjoy lower production and wholesale costs. This enables them to sell their products at a lower price. Additionally, many large businesses can sell their wares at a lower profit margin than smaller companies because their high volume of sales makes up that difference. To be the most competitive among their peers, they must bring the lowest prices to the consumer. The biggest food markets and businesses (like Costco, Walmart, and Amazon) that sell foods and other goods, control so much of the market share that they have the power, and they use it, to dictate the terms of the contracts they offer to their suppliers. In the end, they devalue the products they sell, thereby devaluing the manufacturers of those products we enjoy, the authors of the books we read, the laborers making the clothes we wear and the furniture we buy, and the farmers who grow our food.

How much are we, as consumers, willing to pay for the things that enhance our lives? How much are we willing to pay for the food we eat? In an article by Eliza Barclay on the NPR website, USDA agriculture economist, Annette Clauson, relates that when it comes to consumer purchases, Americans spend the least on food consumed at home compared to just about every other country in the world: "We are purchasing more food for less money, and we are purchasing our food for less of our income." My neighbor dairyman Regli describes, "a cheap food policy versus what is safe and healthy," when referring to the government and strong food lobbying groups that drive decreasing prices for commodities and all the industrial food products and by-products made from them. This also helps to shape the consumer's expectation for cheap food. The chain of consumer demand for cheaper goods can only be broken by the consumer. But how can that happen when so many of us with low- and middle-class incomes struggle to make ends meet? Our fixed costs for healthcare, childcare, transportation, housing, and other necessities are so high for so many that we've inadvertently become a consumer populace that supports unfair conditions for many workers and producers, in our own country and around the globe, with our continuing demand for "sales" and cheap pricing. How is it that we seem to demand and expect so little from our government, the big businesses that influence it, and our current subsidy and tax structures, and yet demand and expect so much from our fellow laborers and producers. If we want to support small and medium-sized businesses and family farms, then we must advocate for measures to help them, pay them for their hard work and often superior products, and help safeguard their very survival.

Farmland is at risk as well; it has become a market commodity. The USDA notes that roughly 30% of our farmland is no longer owned by farmers, but by global and domestic investors. This has contributed to its significant rise in value. According to the Iowa State University Farmland Value Survey, in 1970, farmland in that region sold for $419 per acre. By 2016, the price per acre was $7,183. According to the Oakland Institute, nearly half of all U.S. farmland will change hands in the next 20 years as more farmers retire: "With an estimated $10 billion in capital already looking for access to U.S. farmland, institutional investors openly hope to expand their holdings as this retirement bulge takes place."

Why are so many siblings unwilling to take over the reins on their family's farms? The laborious work might be one reason, but surely the money the family can make by selling their property would be another. Increased flooding and drought conditions, and the lack of profitable opportunity and sales outside of corporate contracts, can certainly dampen enthusiasm for the profession as well. How will a young generation of farmers survive or be able to purchase and operate farmland in such an environment? How can our government ensure the long-term protection of the "hands-on" family farm (and because the home real estate market is running a parallel course, how can they also protect working-class homeownership)? How may we, as consumers, initiate change in the marketplace to benefit our country's farmers and laboring class, indeed family farmers and laboring classes everywhere? These would be excellent subjects to explore at a Neighborhood Café.

It seems likely that if we don't insist on certain changes to our current economic system, our buying behaviors will continue to eliminate many more small businesses of all kinds and we will end up with a handful of companies that will control all retail markets. Often, as consumers, we believe we are supporting small, mid-sized, and local businesses when we purchase some of the products we take home with us. Retaining varying degrees of autonomy, many of those companies have long since been bought up by one of the dozen conglomerates that dominate our global food marketplace. In a 2013 report, "Behind The Brands," Oxfam International describes the climate where these mighty businesses thrive: "Their policies, and the ones they help write for governments have enormous influence over the diets and working conditions of people worldwide, and on the environment." Certainly big business has a place in the world but we must redefine their lawful place and negate their current ability to redefine ours. Although such monopolies are detrimental when left unchecked, I believe that the power these companies wield, their supply chains, resources, and the infrastructure they have in place, may also represent an opportunity to make sweeping positive changes when addressing many of the urgent challenges we face today; we can already see that beginning to happen. Currently, however, the continued monopoly-forming (illegal when I was young) mergers and acquisitions too often produce a landscape that reflects the frustrations echoed by many in the organic agricultural industry. What does that landscape look like?

Jim Regli describes how, "Smaller farmers who spend a tremendous amount of time and resources to maintain their organic and animal welfare certifications watch large businesses hire lawyers and nutritionists to help them skirt organic pasture requirements," and other regulations. As big business enters the organic food market, continues Regli, they also "hire lobbyists to constantly pressure Congress and our lawmakers to weaken the rules for organic production." Long-delayed stocking density and outdoor access protections for livestock that were to be required for organic certification, but were rolled back instead, are examples of such interference. On the Bloomberg news website, authors Martin and Singh write, "Some organic farmers have become so frustrated by the direction of the government's organic program they have come up with their own enhanced standards, called the "Real Organic Project," and they plan on adding their seal on food labels in addition to the USDA seal. Dave Chapman, farmer and executive director of the project states, "We are not trying to undermine the National Organic Program. We are trying to save it."

Mark Kastel, co-founder of The Cornucopia Institute (which promotes the "good food movement") stated to CNBC that "We've had a full frontal assault by corporate agribusiness that's decided to invest in organics...The majority of farmers are doing it right. What our concerns are is the USDA is too friendly with corporate agribusiness and really not doing a judicious job enforcing the law." He also notes the problem isn't necessarily about the size of an operation, but the intent of its owners. "These aren't matters of corporate scale," he says on bloombergnews.com, but "a matter of corporate ethics."

The Cornucopia Institute is an advocacy group within the organic industry. According to their website, cornucopia.org, they "research, issue, and promote findings based in science that are fundamental to maintaining the integrity of organic labeling, production, processing, and marketing." They provide information to family farmers and consumers, and many of their staff members have deep roots in agriculture and the organic movement. "Watchdog" organizations help us in many ways, but it is the consumer who has the last word. As "ordinary" people in our country, we might feel helpless to change the system, but in truth, we can initiate change as we have in the past. We have power over the biggest companies when we decide what we will purchase and what we will not, and when united we have a powerful voice to drive change in government, including our current pro-corporate leaning judiciary.

There are strategies that are effective means for change, on their own and especially when in concert with other tactics, like consumer boycotts, other forms of peaceful resistance, and peaceful support, as well. On the teenVOGUE website, Amit Thakkar, founder and CEO of LawMaker, recommends committing 15 minutes a week to stay on top of your local, state, and federal officials by writing or phoning them, and becoming more informed and involved in your local political landscape where we have the most power to effect change. Thakkar also stresses, "stop sharing fake news [which] derives power from the use of the share button...verify what you're reading by checking other sources such as snopes. If you can't find verification, or don't want to spend the time, don't share the news...Everything we do online is measured and monetized...Each time we click on a headline, that outlet receives data about us." We're also sending a signal that we want to read more of the same types of stories, so, Thakkar continues, "click wisely...and focus more on learning rather than always being right... your goal shouldn't be to change [peoples] minds, but to hear the core of their thinking and gain a better understanding of how the same topic impacts people with different views and life circumstances." She also suggests complementing our local officials when they do something to assist us: "Positive reinforcement is shown to influence our behavior more than negative reinforcement, [so] call their offices, send emails, or even donate as little as $10 – these are great ways to incentivize the type of behavior you want to see from your elected officials." I'll add that those actions also allow them to see that we're paying attention to the job they're doing. Thakkar ends her op-ed by highlighting the importance of focusing on solutions: "Proposing informed solutions empowers all of us."

Another tactic we can use to foster progress might involve pressuring the big grocery store chains to invest in the integrity of our food chain, passing along some of the millions of dollars in annual profits that they make through our patronage. As an example: by establishing a lower than usual mark-up on all fresh "organic" meats, poultry, eggs, and produce, sustainably wild-caught and sustainably farmed fish, they can promote their altruism by passing on a "good will" discount to their customers. How might a program like that be practical for food markets?

The standard supermarket chains earn much of their profits from their large volume of sales. According to "CSIMarket.com," typical net profit margins for the conventional grocery industry run in the mid-1 percent to mid-2 percent range, less even than restaurants. These low figures reflect their average "shrink level," the loss of product primarily due to theft and perishable food spoilage (averaging 30%). These factors contribute to lower profits for the markets and increased prices for the consumer. On the USDA website, 2010 annual national figures showed that for that year alone, "31 percent food loss at the retail and consumer levels corresponded to approximately 133 billion pounds and $161 billion worth of food." The United Nations currently estimates that more than one-third of food produced worldwide is lost or wasted. Most of the unused food ends up in landfills and is a major producer of the greenhouse gas, methane. Every year, vast quantities of land, water, chemicals, and fossil fuels are used to grow that food. Even with these disturbing statistics, perishable food waste continues to grow. One contributing factor is consumer demand for choice; we want to see abundant displays of fresh food in the markets we patronize.

However, the food need not be wasted. A lot of struggling families can be fed on those foods before they go bad; additionally, consumers can avoid food waste at home and lower their weekly grocery expenditures. In restaurants where I've worked, and in my own home as well, I generally prepare a "clean out the refrigerator" meal or soup once a week in which I cook everything before it spoils. These creative meals often turn out to be my favorites to construct and eat. In a supermarket, food deemed unsellable because it's past its prime can be donated to local food banks and non-profit kitchens. However, with net profit margins so low for most food markets, how might they profit from the donations to justify and support a "good will" discount for its customers? One way to lower organic food prices for consumers and address food waste might look like this: currently, tax-payers are indirectly subsidizing fast food, and other corporate giants, costing us billions of dollars annually. Our tax code allows CEO "performance pay" to be a deductible expense; it also gifts other "special tax breaks" on the federal, state, and local levels that significantly reduce these companies' annual tax liabilities. Reigning in the most excessive hand-outs could help support a "good will" discount and other needed reforms. A portion of the taxes generated could be redirected to pay supermarkets for all past prime but unspoiled foods that they donate. Supermarkets would not only have to document and verify their tax-deductible charity but a substantial designated percentage of the money received would go to support a "good will" discount on all fresh organic foods and humanely-raised meats. This plan would benefit the markets, their customers, and those who need more access to nourishing food; everyone would benefit except those companies that possess the means to pay their fair share of taxes. With the additional revenue, this represents another opportunity to work together with business and government to solve a number of problems we face today. Many of the significant beneficial changes that we'd like to see in the local and global marketplace depend on the involvement, cooperation, and even the direction of the consumer.

An alternative strategy food markets can employ to bring down the retail cost of fresh organic foods and humanely-raised meats would balance a lower profit margin on those perishables with an increased profit margin on goods such as soft drinks, cakes, candy, and the most highly refined unhealthy foods. When I priced menu items in my restaurant kitchens, I typically charged more than the usual mark-up on lower-end foods such as pasta dishes, while charging less than the usual mark-up on high-end steaks and seafood entrees. Priced to sell, my menus made expensive meals accessible to more of my customers and helped me provide fresher meals for everyone because of a more even rotation of products. Whenever I visit a conventional supermarket for something unavailable at my local health food stores, I generally look at their organic offerings. Often, the fruits and vegetables don't look as fresh as the conventionally grown produce. Adjusted pricing (and more use of those organic foods in their deli sections) would help alleviate this problem by generating a more robust turnover of fresh organic goods. Modifying mark-ups is not an uncommon practice in the food business and it has always made sense to me.

Additionally, we can demand that our government simplify and clarify our food labeling and certifying criteria. It remains time-consuming and difficult to make sense of food labels, to discover the difference between truth and mere marketing. Attempts to change the status quo are often blocked by food industry lobbying groups in Washington D.C., and in all states that have a label reform bill on their legislative agenda. A typically used strategy is industry's outcry that if forced to comply with added transparency and labeling changes, food prices will soar for the consumer because of their increased financial burden; and yet companies commonly change their labels, food prices continue to rise regardless (or the packaging gets smaller), and millions of dollars continue to be invested annually to fight new legislation reforms.

Researching labeling laws and certifications for this book proved immensely frustrating. Because most marketing claims have no legal definitions monitored by the government, food companies can essentially set their own standards for claims like "natural" and "all-natural," "free-range," "minimally-processed," "humanely-raised or handled", "ethically (responsibly, sustainably, thoughtfully, or naturally) produced", even "family-farmed," without any proof or third-party verification. The companies that spend the money to adhere to their claims and obtain third-party verification are compromised by this lack of regulation. These terms, and others, remain ill-defined and convoluted, often arbitrary, unenforceable, and unconfirmed. Many consumers seek out "natural" food labels, often because they mistakenly believe that such foods are produced organically, without hormones, steroids, antibiotics, pesticides, herbicides, or genetically modified organisms. But "natural" and "all-natural" means only that producers added no artificial ingredients and colorings to the final product. For meat and poultry, according to the USDA website, "minimal processing" represents another requirement, although the definition of this term remains ambiguous as well. Additionally, the "all-natural" claim means nothing in terms of animal welfare or healthful attributes. The USDA regulates fresh meats, poultry, and egg products, the FDA, all other foods. According to truthinadvertising. org (and confirmed on the FDA website), the FDA acknowledges "that it did not address food production methods, such as the use of pesticides, or food processing or manufacturing methods, such as pasteurization or irradiation, when it formed its policy on natural...or whether the term 'natural' should describe any nutritional or other health benefit." The USDA doesn't define "natural" at all.

Given this lack of clarity, I should explain that when I describe something as "sustainable" I refer to a product or a process that can endure over time using techniques that allow for long-term ecological balance. And when I describe something as "green," "ecologically sound," "eco- or environmentally-friendly," or "clean," I mean that it has minimal negative impacts on, and maximum benefits for the environment, including the people and wildlife affected by it. These terms, when used for marketing purposes, may possess more "adaptable" interpretations, or perhaps mean nothing at all. This is not only damaging to companies that are spending their resources to produce a more ethical and healthy product but to the consumers who are being misled.

Because of the vague definitions and varied nature of our current labeling laws, consumers can best judge most food products by taking little notice of brand names and healthy ingredients touted on the front cover (both can be misleading), and marketing slogans like multi-grain which doesn't necessarily mean whole-grain. Focus instead on the ingredients list and nutritional facts, looking specifically for high fiber content, no trans fats, and low proportions of saturated fats, sodium, and added sugars. Daily Value (DV) represents the percentage of a particular nutrient present per stated serving size in relation to what the total daily intake of that nutrient should be according to FDA guidelines. The American Heart Association website specifies that for an average diet of 2,000 calories per day, more than 20% of the Daily Value per serving is high, while 5% or less is low. Individual needs, adjusted for age, height, weight, and level of activity, will vary.

Look for specific certification seals. Third-party certifications generally represent the most safeguards for animals. Conditions also improve with certain government regulated protections, as for "cage-free" eggs and "grass-fed" ruminants, and I encourage their support, as well. However, even these upgraded standards don't go far enough, and conditions at most factory farms remain horrendously cruel, characterized by high stocking density, ill-treatment of animals, and unhealthy environments for workers. The marketing images used to picture happy livestock grazing peacefully in pastoral settings bear no relationship to the reality of factory farms. Such marketing images are used to suppress the rather bleak and disturbing truth.

The bewildering number of miscellaneous certification terms and seals add to the confusion when evaluating a product label. I want above all to see one enhanced organic certification that addresses everything I believe most of us want from our food supply: no added hormones and antibiotics, no pesticides and herbicides, minimally-processed products that contain no GMOs or artificial ingredients. The enhancement would come from incorporating whole-systems management on farms based on specific permaculture principles, fostering diversity, rain and energy catchment, water conservation, and waste management. To achieve this "enhanced" organic certification, these foods must also be fair-traded and ethically produced, both workers and livestock protected. These guarantees would all be included in just one overarching designation, "gold standard organic," its certification defined by straightforward, common-sense regulations and sufficient oversight. At present, the only seal that represents the majority of the above claims is the "organic" certification, our most comprehensive certification to date.

Today, corn and soy farmers (and other commodity farmers) receive many government subsidies, and although other factors are involved, this can lead to either a saturation of product or an undersupply in the marketplace, resulting in agribusiness and the government's ability to control global pricing for those commodities. This, in turn, can force many small farmers across the globe off of their lands because they can't compete; many end up migrating elsewhere to earn a living and feed their families, including many in Latin America who seek refuge in our country. If we use those subsidies differently, however, we could instead support our farmers and ranchers engaged in the process of becoming organic-certified, and help already existing organic farmers meet the new "gold" standards.

Our economic systems and tax structure, which favor mono-crop, chemical-intensive farms, too often reward harmful and abusive behavior and penalize beneficial and ethically sound behavior. Perhaps this is one reason why our contemporary society seems more callous and uncivil than in the past: such a backward state of affairs offends people. Of course, the global agricultural marketplace cannot be described in blacks and whites, and, like raising children to behave well and do the right thing, we find moral complexity at every turn. Nonetheless, I believe we can formulate effective common sense incentives that reward long-term integrity and global health over short-term profits. This would be an excellent topic for a Neighborhood Café.

Improving the food we eat, and the markets that bring this food to our tables, would enhance our fitness and create a multitude of healthy jobs. This entire process takes time, so the use of the following recipes, and other non- and low-meat preparations, may help sway supermarkets (and all companies linked within our food chain) by decreasing the sales of factory-farmed meats. The first recipes represent meatless entrees, substantial and full of flavor, that contain the same complete protein complex found in meat. Our bodies can't produce these nine essential amino acids on their own. The remaining recipes contain some meat protein but in modest amounts.

RECIPES

Baked Eggs with Feta
Yield: 4 servings

INGREDIENTS

Extra virgin olive oil | 2 tsp.

Tomato, sliced | 1 large or 2 small-medium

Yellow, orange or red bell pepper, sliced thinly into rings | 1/2

Feta cheese, sliced evenly into 8 pieces | 1/2 lb.

Kalamata olives (optional), pitted and quartered | 6

Eggs | 4

Sea salt, crushed red chiles, oregano, and paprika | 1/4 tsp. each

DIRECTIONS

In a round pie pan, rectangular baking dish, or individual ramekins, make 4 pools of oil using 1/2 tsp. per pool. Top each with 2–3 overlapping slices each of tomato and bell pepper; arrange 2 slices of the feta on top of the vegetables, leaving a gap between the slices. Crack an egg into each gap, sprinkle each "bundle" with 1/8 tsp. each of salt, paprika, oregano, and red chile flakes. Bake in a preheated 350-degree oven until the egg white is just set and the yolk is still runny, about 18-22 minutes. Serve on, or with, a bed of room temperature baby spinach (lightly sprinkled with salt, lemon, and oil) and a small, lightly buttered baked potato and/or garlic toast.

Note: This egg dish is best served hot from the oven, so be prepared to sit and enjoy it right away!

To make garlic toast: toast, or grill, slices of French or Italian bread until lightly browned. Meanwhile, in a small bowl, mix 2 large peeled and halved garlic cloves and 1 Tbsp. olive oil. With a fork, rub each slice of toast with an oil-coated garlic half. Dip clove back in oil and rub thoroughly into bread again.

Eggplant Jarlsberg with Ricotta Toast

Yield: 3 servings

INGREDIENTS

Tomato sauce | 1–8 oz. can

Garlic, chopped fine | 3

Sea salt | 3/4 tsp.

Oregano, red chile flakes, and thyme | 1/2 tsp. each

Black pepper | 1/4 tsp.

Extra virgin olive oil | 1-1/2 tsp.

Unpeeled Italian purple eggplant, 6 diagonal 1-1/4" slices | 1

Mushrooms, quartered | 12

Jarlsberg and Romano cheeses, grated | 1/2 cup each

Ricotta| 2/3 cup

Basil leaves, rolled and sliced | 1/3 cup

Crusty peasant bread, lightly toasted | 3 slices

Baby spinach | 2 handfuls

DIRECTIONS

In a small bowl, mix the tomato sauce, 2 of the cloves of chopped garlic, 1/4 tsp. each of salt, thyme, oregano, chiles, and 1/8 tsp. pepper. Over medium heat, sauté the eggplant and mushrooms in the oil. Sprinkle with 1/4 tsp. each of salt and thyme, and 1/8 tsp. of pepper. When golden brown (approximately 5 minutes), flip over the eggplant. Spoon the seasoned tomato sauce evenly over eggplant slices, and then sprinkle with an even layer of the grated cheeses. Cover, turn the heat down to low, cook for 8 minutes, or until cheese is melted and eggplant is just tender when pierced with a fork. Meanwhile, rinse the bowl you used to mix the tomato sauce, shake out excess water, add and mix the ricotta, 1/4 cup basil, and the remaining chopped garlic, 1/4 tsp. of salt, and 1/8 tsp. of pepper; spread on the lightly toasted bread. Plate 2 eggplant slices, slightly overlapping, on a bed of spinach. Serve with ricotta toast; garnish with remaining basil.

Lentil and Potato Stew
Yield: 4 – 6 servings

This simple, delicious, and comforting dish is based on a recipe from Karen Lee's excellent cookbook, "The Occasional Vegetarian."

INGREDIENTS

Lentils | 1-1/2 cups
Water | 6 cups
Large onion, 1" dice | 1
Potatoes, 1" dice | 2
Celery stalks | 2
Carrots | 1/2" rounds on the bias | 2
    (3-4, if small)

Sea salt and black pepper | 1/2 tsp.
    each
Ground ginger, cumin, and turmeric | 1
    tsp. each
Olive oil | 1-1/4 Tbsp.
Soy sauce | 1/4 cup
Cabbage (or other leafy green),
    shredded or roughly chopped | 2-1/4
    cups

DIRECTIONS

Warm oil in a large pot over low-medium heat and add the spices. Stir until fragrant, 1–2 minutes. Add the water and remaining ingredients, except the cabbage. Bring to a boil, lower the heat, cover the pot, and simmer for approximately 45 minutes, or until lentils are just tender. Stir in cabbage and cook for 2-3 minutes longer.

VARIATION

For **Lentils with Salmon**, season one small fillet per person, lightly with salt and pepper; place atop the stew during the last 10 or so (depending on the salmon's thickness) minutes of the stew's cooking time. Re-cover the pot and continue to simmer; when the fish is just cooked through, place the salmon atop a small handful of baby spinach or arugula on a wide shallow bowl (or a plate with a high rim). Raise the heat under the pot and stir the cabbage into it; cover again. While waiting 2 minutes for the cabbage to cook, cut a thick wedge of lemon per serving, place it alongside the fish, and spoon the stew aside both.

Stuffed Acorn Squash

Yield: 2 servings

INGREDIENTS

Extra virgin olive oil | 2 tsp.

Onion, 1/4" dice | 1/2

Mushrooms, thinly sliced | 3/4 cup

Sea salt | 1/2 tsp.

Ground black pepper and nutmeg | 1/8 tsp. each

Bulgur | 1/2 cup

Milk and water | 3/4 cup each

Acorn squash, stemmed, halved lengthwise, and seeded | 1

Kale and/or chard, 1/2" chopped | 3-1/4 cups

Peas, frozen or fresh | 1/2 cup

Grated Romano or Jarlsberg cheese or crumbled Feta | 1/2 cup

DIRECTIONS

Lightly salt and pepper squash. Roast, cut side down on a greased sheet pan, in a preheated 375-degree oven for 40-45 minutes, or until just tender. Meanwhile, warm oil and sauté onion and mushrooms with 1/4 tsp. salt over low-medium heat for 4 min. Stir in bulgur, milk, water, remaining 1/4 tsp. salt, black pepper, and nutmeg. Cover and cook on low heat for 10 minutes. Stir in the chopped greens. Cover, turn off the heat, and allow to sit 10-15 minutes, or until the bulgur is just tender. Stir in peas. Remove squash from oven, turn halves cut side up. Stuff cavities with the bulgur mixture; sprinkle with grated cheese. Bake for another 10 minutes until heated through and the cheese is melted. Plate squash atop a handful of lightly dressed arugula or spinach.

VARIATIONS

I enjoy this dish with roasted celery. Cut 3 (or 2 large) celery stalks into 1/2" slices on the bias. Toss in a bowl with 1/4 tsp. salt, 1/8 tsp. each of pepper and thyme, and 1 tsp. each of olive oil and lemon juice or balsamic vinegar. Remove the roasting cut-side down squash from the oven after 25 minutes and scatter the celery (in a single layer) around the halves. Return to the oven for approximately 15 minutes longer, or until squash is just tender. Proceed as directed above. Finish cooking the celery with the stuffed squash.

The bulgur mixture makes an excellent all-purpose stuffing or base to add other ingredients. For stuffed mushrooms, I halve the stuffing recipe (for a small get-to-gether), using mostly mushroom stems in the mix. I stuff the caps, top them with a small piece of Proscuitto that fits the mushrooms, and bake them on a buttered sheet pan at 400 degrees for 15-20 minutes. If I use grated Romano cheese to top the mushrooms, I'll add it the last 6-7 minutes of baking time.

Klara's Cabbage Pancakes

Yield: 2 servings

INGREDIENTS

Green cabbage, shredded by quarters | 4 cups

Snap peas, halved crosswise on the diagonal | 1-1/2 cups

Eggs | 4

Cold water | 1/4 cup

Whole wheat pastry flour | 2 Tbsp.

Sea salt | 1/2 tsp.

Ground black pepper | 1/4 tsp.

Extra virgin olive or sesame oil | 1-1/2 tsp.

Tamari or soy sauce | 2 tsp. plus 2 Tbsp.

Juice of fresh lime or lemon, or vinegar | 2 tsp. plus 2 tsp.

Crushed red chile flakes and Tabasco sauce | 1/4 - 1/3 tsp. each

Honey | 2 tsp.

*Cooked cilantro rice

DIRECTIONS

In a bowl, mix the eggs, flour, water, salt and pepper, and 2 tsp. each of tamari and lime. Stir in cabbage and snap peas; let rest while preparing the sauce. Combine remaining tamari and lime, the chile flakes, Tabasco, and honey in a small serving bowl. Let sit on the stovetop to warm the honey, and stir again before serving. Warm oil in a well-seasoned or non-stick 12" pan. Add cabbage mixture and cook over medium heat until nicely browned, about 5 minutes. Divide into quarters and flip each quarter over with a spatula. Cook 4-5 minutes, and when set, overlap 2 pieces onto each plate. Serve with the sauce and *steamed or boiled rice, to which a pinch of salt and butter, and roughly chopped cilantro has been added at the end of cooking time.

Pasta with Vegetables
Yield: 3 servings

INGREDIENTS

Extra virgin olive oil | 2 tsp.

Small onion, 3/4" dice | 1 (approx. 1 cup)

Garlic cloves, chopped | 6

Sea salt | 1/2 tsp. plus 3/4 tsp.

Dried sage and crushed red chile flakes | 1 tsp. each

Small butternut squash, stem end, 3/4" dice | 2-1/4 cups

Water | 1-1/4 cups

Green beans, cut crosswise on bias in half or thirds | 4-5 oz.

Yellow squash, 1/4" diagonal rounds, halved | 1 (2-1/4 cups)

Juice from lemons | 1-1/2 (3 Tbsp.)

Swiss chard or kale, chopped | 6-8 leaves (4 cups), *set stems aside

Peas | 1 cup

Butter | 1 Tbsp.

Pasta of choice | 1/2 lb.

Grated Romano cheese | 3/4 - 1 cup

DIRECTIONS

Put water to a boil in a large pot (salt well just before adding pasta). Meanwhile, warm oil and sauté onion, garlic, and spices in a medium-large saucepan over medium-low heat for 2 minutes. Add squash with water to barely cover. Simmer, covered, 12 minutes, and then slightly smash the squash. Stir in the beans. Bring back to boil; simmer, partially covered, 5 minutes. Stir in zucchini; bring back to simmer, cover, and shut heat. Place peas and greens in the colander. Right before draining al dente pasta, set aside 1/2 cup of pasta water, stir lemon juice into the vegetable sauce, and turn the heat back on to high. Drain pasta over vegetables in the colander. Stir butter into the sauce until it emulsifies, adding enough pasta water, if needed, to make a light- to medium-bodied sauce. Shut heat, add pasta, greens, and peas, and coat with the sauce. Plate, and serve hot, along with the cheese on the side.

VARIATION

I enjoy this dish with sliced mushrooms (sautéed with the onions) and *trimmed green swiss chard or kale stems (for their crunchy texture), sliced in 1/4" - 1/3" diagonal cuts, and added to the sauce with the zucchini.

RECIPES

Peperoni e Pomodoro alla Maurizio

Yield: 4 servings

My "foodie" brother, Harold, describes his friend Maurizio as "one of the three best amateur chefs that I know." The following represents what Maurizio calls his take on a very simple traditional dish.

INGREDIENTS

Extra virgin olive oil | 2 Tbsp. plus 1 tsp.

Onion, finely chopped | 1

Large red bell peppers, quartered, seeded, sliced very thinly | 2

Tomatoes, in juice (preferably San Marzano) | 1–28 oz. can

Sea salt | 1/2 tsp.

Ground black pepper | 1/4 tsp.

Tarragon | 1/2 tsp. (or 1/4 tsp. ea. basil and thyme)

Eggs | 4

Gruyere, chopped (or grated Parmesan) | 3/4 cup

DIRECTIONS

In a heavy pot, warm oil and sauté onions and peppers over medium heat for 3 minutes, stirring to thoroughly coat the vegetables with the oil. Add seasonings, reduce the heat to medium-low, and stir occasionally for about 10-15 minutes. When onions are translucent, add the tomato juice from the can, and crush the tomatoes by hand in a bowl; add to the pot. Bring to a boil, lower the heat, cover the pot, and cook at a bare simmer, stirring occasionally, for approximately 35-40 minutes; the vegetables should appear almost indistinguishable from each other. Crack eggs into the pan, leaving them intact atop the sauce. Cover the pot and cook for 3-1/2 - 4 minutes, or until the egg whites are just set and the yolks are still runny. If desired, after 2-1/2 minutes, uncover, carefully spread the whites out a bit with a spoon to hasten their cooking (just to be sure they cook through before the yolks overcook), and re-cover the pot for the last minute or so. Meanwhile, divide cheese among 4 individual serving bowls and get everyone around the table to enjoy this dish while hot. Carefully ladle sauce over the cheese and top with an egg. Serve with garlic toast (see recipe for Baked Eggs with Feta) or with fresh crusty Italian bread.

French Lentil and Vegetable Stew
Yield: 4 servings

INGREDIENTS

Extra virgin olive oil | 2 tsp.

Onion, halved lengthwise, 3/4" dice | 1

Celery stalks, 3/4" dice | 2

Carrots, 3/4" dice | 2

Small turnip, 3/4" dice | 1

Potato, 3/4" dice | 1 lg. or 3 small

Garlic cloves, peeled, thinly sliced | 4

Sea salt | 1 tsp. plus an additional 1 tsp.

Ground black pepper, dry mustard, and thyme | 1/2 tsp. each

Bay leaves | 2

Mushrooms, quartered | 12

Tomato sauce (preferably just tomatoes and salt)| 1–4 oz. can

Chicken or vegetable broth | 4 cups

Dry red wine and water | 1 cup each

French green (or brown) lentils | 1-1/2 cups

Green cabbage or kale, 1" chunks | 2 cups

Red wine vinegar | 1-1/2 Tbsp.

Romano cheese, grated | 4 oz.

DIRECTIONS

Warm the oil over medium heat. Sauté the next five ingredients with 1 tsp. salt for 8 minutes. Lower heat to low-medium; stir in garlic, herbs and mushrooms, and cook for approximately 3 minutes. Add tomato sauce, remaining salt, broth, wine, water and lentils. Bring to a boil, cover, and simmer 55-65 minutes for green (less for brown), or until the lentils are just tender. Add cabbage and vinegar, cook for 3-4 minutes. Serve hot in bowls; top with cheese. Serve with crusty french bread.

VARIATION

Omit cheese and serve over rice.

Stewed Mushrooms in Paprika Sauce
Yield: 3 servings

INGREDIENTS

Olive oil and butter | 1-1/2 tsp. each
White or crimini mushrooms | 1 lb.
Onion and large carrot, diced | 1 each
Garlic cloves, finely chopped | 3
Sea salt | 1-1/4 tsp.
Ground black pepper and crushed red
   chile flakes | 1/4 tsp. each
Caraway seed | 1/2 tsp.
Sweet paprika (Hungarian, if available)
   | 2-1/2 Tbsp.

Flour | 1 Tbsp.
Dry red wine | 2/3 cup
Diced tomatoes, in juice | 1 - 15 oz. can
Water | 1/3 cup
Beef or mushroom broth | 2 cups
Bell pepper, quartered, seeded, and
   sliced | 1
*Sour cream or Greek yogurt | 1/3 cup
Boiled new potatoes or egg noodles

DIRECTIONS

Warm oil in a large pot over medium heat and add onion. Sauté for 3 minutes. Add mushrooms, carrot, and seasonings and continue cooking for 2 minutes, careful not to burn the spices. Stir in the flour and cook for an additional 2 minutes, stirring frequently. Add the wine; stir well for 1-2 minutes to deglaze the pan, and add the broth and tomatoes. Rinse the tomato can with the third cup of water and add to the pot; stir in bell pepper. Raise heat, bring to a boil, lower heat, and simmer, partially covered, for approximately 20 minutes. Meanwhile, boil potato cubes or egg noodles. Serve mushrooms and sauce over the potatoes or noodles. Top with a dollop of sour cream or yogurt (preferably Greek).

Notes: A simple vinegared cucumber salad goes well with this meal. See recipe index for Cucumber, Cauliflower, and Bean Salad. If desired, use that dressing recipe and add only cucumber and onion.

If you have leftover sauce, it makes a delicious stuffing for an omelette. Reduce, first, to a medium-thick consistency, if necessary.

*Daisy brand light sour cream, available nationally, is an excellent rich-tasting low-fat sour cream without added chemicals. I highly recommend it for this recipe, or other similar product.

Red Beans and Rice with Beef and Bok Choy
Yield: 2 – 3 servings

Although there are similar ingredients, this is not a traditional southern "red beans and rice", nor an "Asian-style beef and bok choy" dish. However, it stands on its own as one of many humble and comforting meals.

INGREDIENTS
Extra virgin olive oil | 1 tsp. plus an additional 1 tsp.
Turmeric, and sweet paprika or annatto | 1/2 tsp. each
White and brown Basmati rice | 1/3 cup each
Chicken broth or water | 1 cup
Onion and carrot, 1/4" dice | 3/4 cup each
Sea salt | 1/2 tsp. plus 1/4 tsp. for rice
Garlic cloves, finely chopped | 2
Ground beef (or meat of your choice) | 1/3 – 1/2 lb.

Crushed chile flakes, thyme, and additional sea salt | 1/2 tsp. ea.
Black pepper | 1/8 tsp.
Plum tomatoes (fresh, if available), 1/4" dice | 2 (3/4 - 1 cup)
White wine, broth, water, or a combination | 1/2 cup
Drained kidney beans | 1 – 15 oz. can
Bok choy | 3/4" dice | 3 cups
Snap (or snow) peas, stem ends trimmed, halved crosswise | 2 cups

DIRECTIONS

In a small saucepan with a tight-fitting lid, warm 1 tsp. of oil, stir in the paprika or annatto, and turmeric; add the rice and stir to coat. Stir in 1 cup of broth or water; bring to a simmer. Cover, cook over low heat for 20 minutes. Without lifting the lid, let sit for 10 minutes or so. Meanwhile, in a medium skillet over medium heat, sauté the onion, carrot, and 1/2 tsp. of salt in remaining tsp. of oil for 3-4 minutes. Stir in the garlic and cook for 1 minute; add the beef, black pepper, 1/2 tsp. each of salt, chile flakes, and thyme. Blend together as you break up the beef with the back of a wooden spoon. Cook until meat loses most of its pink color; if the meat exudes excess grease, pour most of it out, discarding it safely. Add the tomato; deglaze the pan with the remaining 1/2 cup of liquid, stirring well to incorporate the bits from the bottom of the pan. Add the beans, bring to a simmer, cover, and cook for 6 minutes over low heat. Stir in bok choy and snap peas; cover and cook for 1-1/2 - 2 minutes (if using snow peas, wait and add them the last minute of cooking time). Add 1/4 tsp. of salt to the rice, and stir into bean mixture; serve with a green salad.

Roasted Tuna Piccante

Yield: 2 servings

When Joe and I had our restaurant, Squisi's, we served this sauce over chargrilled trout stuffed with fresh spinach. The salsa piccante is also delicious spooned over chargrilled oysters, salmon, scallops, chicken, eggplant, summer squash, and portobello mushrooms. It makes a great dressing for potato, pasta, and bean salads. It can be prepared ahead of time and will last all week in the fridge. Bring to room temperature, and stir well, before using.

INGREDIENTS

Tuna steaks, 4-5 oz. each (approximately 1" thick) | 2
Chard leaves, stem removed | 2
Mushrooms, quartered | 6
Small-medium cauliflower florets | 1 cup
Zucchini or yellow squash, in 1/2" diagonal rounds | 1 cup
Sea salt | 1/2 tsp.
Extra virgin olive oil | 1 tsp.
Room temperature baby greens | 2 small handfuls

SALSA PICCANTE

(halve the recipe if you don't want leftover sauce)
Extra virgin olive oil | 3 Tbsp.
Fresh lemon juice | 1 Tbsp. plus 1 tsp.
Balsamic vinegar | 1 Tbsp.
Sea salt | 2/3 tsp.
Black pepper and oregano | 1/4 tsp. each
Capers | 1 scant Tbsp.
Green onion, thinly sliced | 1/4 cup
Parsley, finely chopped | 1/4 cup
Fresh roasted red bell peppers (peeled, seeded, finely chopped) | 2 (or 2/3 cup jarred, drained, and finely chopped)

DIRECTIONS

Prepare the **Salsa Piccante**: slightly warm the oil; add the lemon juice, vinegar, oregano, capers, salt, and pepper. Remove from heat. Combine the prepared green onion, parsley, and roasted pepper in a medium bowl. Place a damp cloth underneath the bowl to keep it from sliding across the counter. Very gradually, whisk in the warmed oil mixture until the sauce is emulsified. Let it sit at room temperature. Grease sheet pan (or parchment-lined sheet pan) with 1/2 tsp. olive oil. Place chard leaves towards the middle of the pan, keeping them separate. Top each leaf with a tuna steak. Spread mushrooms, florets, and squash around the fish. Sprinkle the fish and vegetables with the 1/2 tsp. of salt and remaining tsp. of oil. Roast in a preheated 450-degree oven for 8 minutes, or until the tuna is almost cooked through (it's center still slightly pink – or cook it a bit less, if desired). Plate fish on a small bed of baby greens, and the vegetables alongside. Mix salsa piccante well, spoon over fish, and drizzle over the vegetables.

Easy Chicken and Rice
Yield: 2 servings

INGREDIENTS
Brown and white Basmati rice | 3/4 cup total

Small onion, chopped, 1/4" dice | 1

Small-medium carrot, chopped. 1/4" dice | 1

Small celery stalk, chopped, 1/4" dice | 1

Mushrooms, sliced | 8

Garlic cloves, chopped | 3

Sea salt | 1 tsp.

Cayenne and black pepper | 1/8 tsp. each

Thyme and dry mustard | 1/2 tsp. each

Chicken thighs, bone-in, skin on | 2

*Chicken broth | 2-1/4 cups

Frozen peas, thawed | 2/3 cup

Chopped fresh parsley | 1/4 cup

DIRECTIONS
*If your container of broth is a bit shy of 2-1/4 cups, make up the difference with water.

Combine all the vegetables and herbs, except for the peas and parsley, in a greased 9x5" loaf pan. Add the broth and gently stir to mix the ingredients well. Press chicken pieces into the mixture to partially submerge. Cover the pan tightly and bake in a preheated 350-degree oven for 1 hour. Uncover, increase temperature to 400 degrees, and cook for approximately 25 minutes, or until top is golden brown. Let sit, partially, but primarily, covered, for 6-8 minutes to allow juices to settle into the rice. Plate the chicken; with a fork, stir room temperature peas and parsley into the rice, and serve alongside the chicken.

Salmon with Black Beans and Yellow Squash

Yield: 3 servings

INGREDIENTS

Salmon fillets, 4–5 oz. each | 3

Sea salt | 3/4 tsp. plus 1/8 tsp.

Oregano, basil | 1/8 tsp. each

Coriander (optional) | 1/8 tsp.

Black pepper | 1/4 tsp

Red chile flakes | 1/2 tsp.

Extra virgin olive oil | 2 tsp. plus an
    additional 1-1/2 tsp.

Water | 1/3 cup plus additional 1/4 cup

Green onions | 1 bunch

Dijon mustard | 1 Tbsp.

Limes | 2

Black beans| 1–15 oz. can

Carrots, 1/4" diagonal slices | 2 small-
    medium

Celery, 1/4" diagonal slices | 1 large
    stalk

Green bell pepper, quartered and
    sliced 1/4" | 1 small

Yellow squash, halved and sliced 1/4"
    diagonally | 2 small-medium

DIRECTIONS

In a medium saucepan, season 1/3 cup water with 1/4 tsp. salt, the red chiles, oregano, basil, 1/2 tsp. olive oil, and the coriander, if using. Bring to a boil, add carrot and celery, bring to a simmer, cover, and steam 3-4 minutes. Uncover, stir in the beans, and cook for 1 minute; stir in squash, bell pepper, and 1/8 tsp. salt. Cover, cook for 45 seconds - 1 minute longer, turn off the heat, and leave the lid slightly ajar. Meanwhile, in another pan, sauté salmon over medium heat in the remaining 1-1/2 tsp. oil, skin side up. Season with 1/4 tsp. salt and 1/8 tsp. pepper. Cook 1-1/2 minutes, turn the fish over, add the green onion to the bottom of the pan around the fillets, and season the salmon and onion with the remaining 1/4 tsp. salt and 1/8 tsp. pepper. Cook fish according to thickness (10 minutes per inch, or a little less). Four to five minutes before salmon is done, turn the heat under the beans to medium-low. Plate the fillets when they're ready and spoon green onion over one side of each fillet. To the salmon pan, add Dijon, juice of 1-1/2 limes (cut remaining half into 3 wedges and add to the plates), and 1/4 cup water; boil over high heat while scraping the bottom of the pan to deglaze, and pour over fish. Drizzle each fillet with a 1/2 tsp. of olive oil. Plate the hot vegetables and beans alongside them.

Kibbeh Steaks

Yield: 3-4 servings

INGREDIENTS

Bulgur | 2/3 cup
Water | 3/4 cup
Ground lamb (or beef) | 2/3 lb.
Sea salt | 3/4 tsp. plus an additional 3/4 tsp.
Black pepper | 1/8 tsp. plus an additional 1/8 tsp.
Extra virgin olive oil | 2 tsp.
Onion, sliced in thin rings | 1
Mushrooms, sliced | 8

Garlic cloves, chopped | 3
Navy beans, rinsed and drained | 1–15 oz. can
Tomato sauce | 1–8 oz. can
Water | 4 oz. (fill empty tomato sauce can halfway up)
Maple syrup | 2 Tbsp.
Cider vinegar | 1 Tbsp.
Dijon mustard | 1-1/2 tsp.
Baby spinach | 5–6 small handfuls

DIRECTIONS

Bring water to a boil in a covered saucepan. Turn off the heat and stir in the bulgur; cover tightly and let sit for 25 minutes. Uncover, stir, and let cool for 8 minutes or so. In a medium bowl, mix bulgur, ground meat, garlic, and half the salt and pepper. Shape into 4 oblong patties. Heat oil in a large skillet over medium-high heat. Brown the patties on both sides, about 6 minutes total; remove to a large dish. Lower heat to medium, add onions and mushrooms to the same pan, and sauté for 3-4 minutes. Stir in the next 6 ingredients and the remaining salt and pepper. Return patties to the pan; bring to a gentle simmer, cover, and cook for 8–10 minutes longer, or to the desired doneness. Plate each patty on a bed of spinach. With tongs, pick out most of the onion rings from the bean mixture and place them atop the patties. Spoon beans aside the Kibbeh, and pour the remaining sauce over the steaks.

VARIATION

For Spaghetti and Meatballs: Add 1/2 cup grated Parmesan or Romano cheese to the meat mixture. Shape into 12-16 meatballs instead of patties; sear as directed above, and set aside. Omit the navy beans, tomato sauce, and Dijon. Instead, after sautéing the onions and mushrooms for 2 minutes, add 1 large crushed and peeled clove of garlic and cook an additional 1-2 minutes. Add 1–15 oz. can crushed tomatoes in juice (rinse the can with 2-3 Tbsp. of water and add to the pan), the remaining salt and pepper, and 1/2 tsp. of oregano. Decrease cider vinegar and maple syrup to 1 tsp. each, and stir into sauce. Return meatballs and any accumulated juice, stir, bring to a slow simmer, and cook, partially covered, for 20 minutes. Raise heat, if necessary, and reduce to a medium-bodied consistency. Gently stir in 1-1/2 tsp. of butter until blended through. Toss with Spaghetti, or pasta of your choice, and serve with grated Romano or Parmesan and a green salad. Sprinkle pasta with fresh-cut basil or parsley.

Turkey and Chickpea Stew

Yield: 4 servings

INGREDIENTS

Extra virgin olive oil | 2 tsp.

Rosemary, crushed red chiles, and ground black pepper | 1/4 tsp. each

Sea salt, thyme, turmeric | 1/2 tsp. each

Onion, 1/2" dice | 1

Garlic cloves, chopped | 2 lg.

Sweet potatoes, 3/4 " dice | 2

Rutabaga or turnip, 3/4" dice | 1

Dry white wine, and dry sherry or apple juice | 3/4 cup each

Chicken stock | 3 cups

Carrots and celery stalks, 1" dice | 2 - 3 each

Mushrooms, quartered | 6 oz.

Turkey breast fillets, sliced in 1-1/4" diagonals | 1-1/2 lbs.

Additional sea salt | 1 tsp.

Additional thyme | 1/4 tsp.

Chickpeas, rinsed and drained | 1-15 oz. can

Chard or kale, 1-1/4" chunks | 4 - 5 cups

Fresh lemon juice | 1/2 (1 Tbsp.)

DIRECTIONS

Sauté onion and spices (not the additional salt and thyme) in oil over low-medium heat for 2 minutes. Add the garlic and stir 1 minute. Mix in potato and rutabaga, and turn heat to medium-high for 30 seconds. Add white wine, and sherry or juice, and stir from the bottom of the pan for 1 minute. Add broth, bring to a low simmer, cover, and cook for 10 minutes. Add carrots, celery, 1/2 tsp. of salt, and the additional thyme; cover and cook for 12 minutes. Slightly smash some of the vegetables (with a potato masher or back of a big fork or spoon) to slightly thicken the sauce. Stir in the turkey, chickpeas, and remaining 1/2 tsp. of salt. Simmer over low heat, uncovered, for approximately 5 minutes, or until meat is just cooked through. Add the greens and lemon juice; cook for 2 min. Serve hot in bowls.

VARIATION

Use sliced boneless, skinless chicken pieces if turkey fillets are not available. Adjust cooking time, if necessary.

RECIPES

Sausage Braised in Beer
Yield: 4 servings

Most sausages are high in saturated fat and sodium and are not normally considered a healthy meat choice. However, it is affordable, accessible, often delicious, and when eaten in moderation should not be harmful (unless you have a medical condition that would make it otherwise). There are some great-tasting and healthier sausage choices, and you might consider looking for them, but in the end, it's important that you and your family enjoy the flavor and texture. If you can find sausage that uses meat from "certified humanely-raised" and "organic" sources, all the better!

INGREDIENTS
Onion, halved lengthwise and sliced | 1
Small-medium new potatoes, quartered | 8-12 (depending on size)
Turnip or rutabaga, 1" dice | 1
Sweet potato, 1 " dice | 1

Smoked sausage links of your choice, sliced into 4 pieces | 1 lb.

Sea salt, red chile flakes, sweet paprika, and thyme | 1/2 tsp. each

Black pepper, sage, and caraway seed | 1/4 tsp. each

Lager beer | 1-12 oz. bottle

Water | 12 oz.

Carrots, 3/4" diagonal slices | 3

Celery stalks, 3/4" diagonal slices | 2

Green cabbage, 2" wedges | 4

Red wine vinegar, maple syrup, and Dijon | 1 Tbsp. each

Parsley, chopped | 1/3 cup

DIRECTIONS

In a medium-large pot with a lid, layer the first three ingredients. Sprinkle evenly with the spices. Top with sausage and pierce several times with a fork; pour beer and water into the pot. Bring to a simmer, cover, and cook gently for 10 minutes. Stir in carrots, celery, vinegar, syrup, and Dijon. Lay cabbage wedges on top, slightly overlapping thin ends. Press down, slightly, with the back of a spoon. Bring back to a simmer, cover, and cook for 15-20 minutes, or until carrots, celery, and cabbage are cooked al dente. Transfer sausage and vegetables (leaving some white and sweet potatoes in the pot) to large serving bowls. Stir in parsley and mash some of the potatoes into the sauce until slightly thickened. Ladle into the bowls. Offer horseradish and additional mustard, if desired.

Seafood Pasta
Yield: 2 - 3 servings

INGREDIENTS

Extra virgin olive oil | 2 tsp.

Onion, 1/2" dice | 1/2

Garlic cloves, chopped | 3

Leaf thyme, crushed red chiles, fennel seed | 1/2 tsp. each

Sea salt | 1 tsp.

Dry vermouth or white wine | 2/3 cup

Diced tomatoes in juice | 1-15 oz. can (approximately 1-1/2 c.)

Juice from 1 lemon | 2 Tbsp.

*Black mussels, washed | 1-1/2 dozen

*Small clams, washed | 1 dozen

21-25 prawns, peeled and deveined or in shell | 4-6

Parsley, chopped | 1/3 cup

Butter | 2 tsp.

Pasta (I prefer linguine or spaghettini for this dish) | 1/3-1/2 lb.

Reserved pasta water | 1/3 cup

Baby spinach | 2-3 handfuls

DIRECTIONS

Prep all seafood and vegetables. Bring water to a boil in a large pot for the pasta. Meanwhile, in a large skillet with a lid, over medium heat, sauté onion and spices in olive oil for 2-3 minutes. Add garlic, and cook for 1 minute longer. Turn up the heat to medium-high for the last 10 seconds; add vermouth, stir for 30 seconds, and reduce heat to medium-low. Stir in lemon juice and tomato; simmer for 5 minutes. Stir in the shellfish and cover the pan. Meanwhile, line plates with spinach, and drain pasta when al dente. Remove prawns when just cooked through, and the fish as the shells open (about 5 minutes total); place around the perimeter of the plates. Discard any whose shells don't open. Add butter and parsley to the sauce and stir well until blended through. Stir in some reserved pasta water if needed to thin the sauce. Shut fire, add pasta, and mix to coat well. Place noodles in the center of the plate. Pour remaining sauce over pasta and shellfish, and serve immediately.

*Note: To wash, and ensure there's no sand inside the mollusks, clean and rinse their shells as soon as you get back from the market (and pull the "beards" out of the mussels). Keep the shellfish in a bowl, covered with cold salted water, in the refrigerator, until ready to use. Keep them uncovered, at least partially, so they can breathe. It's best to use them within a day. If any shells are at all open, and they don't close after you tap on them a few times, discard them.

Chicken Vegetable Adobo
Yield: 4 servings

INGREDIENTS

Olive oil | 1 tsp.

Bone-in chicken thighs, excess skin removed | 4

Soy sauce and cider vinegar and maple syrup | 1/3 cup each

Water | 1/2 cup

Small onion, finely diced | 1

Garlic cloves, minced | 8

Sea salt | 1/2 tsp. plus additional 1/2 tsp.

Black pepper and cinnamon | 1/2 tsp. each

Bay leaf | 2

Bok choy, 1-1/2" slices | 3 cups

Broccoli florets with 1" of stem | 3 cups

Cooked brown and white Jasmine rice blend | 3 cups

Fresh chopped basil or cilantro (optional) | 1/4 cup

DIRECTIONS

In a container that fits the chicken in a single layer, mix marinade ingredients (soy, vinegar, syrup, water) until blended. Add thighs, skin side up, and marinate at room temp. for 1-1/4 hours, or if longer, covered in the refrigerator. The longer the chicken marinates (up to a day), the more flavor the finished dish will have. In a medium saucepan, warm oil and sauté onion over medium-low heat for 4 minutes. Add garlic, 1/2 tsp. of salt, and the seasonings; cook for 1-1/2 minutes. Pour marinade into the pan and boil until reduced by a quarter. Add chicken, skin side down, cover, and simmer (turning pieces once) for 35-40 minutes, or until chicken is just cooked through at the bone. Without stirring in the vegetables, place broccoli on top of the chicken, add the bok choy on top of the broccoli, and sprinkle with the remaining salt. Cover and steam for 4-5 minutes until almost al dente. Stir in the vegetables to combine with the other ingredients, cover, and cook 30 seconds to 1 minute longer. Plate the chicken and vegetables, leaving as much sauce in the pan as you can. Over high heat, boil 2-4 minutes, or until the sauce thickens and drips a bit slowly from a spoon (add an additional 1/2 to 3/4 tsp. of vinegar, if desired). Meanwhile, remove the skin from the thighs, and top chicken with the herbs, if desired. Divide sauce evenly over chicken and vegetables. Serve with Jasmine rice.

VARIATION

You can include other vegetables when you add the broccoli and bok choy, like sliced mushrooms, and/or 3/4-1" slices of summer squash. If using mushrooms, add them before you layer in the other vegetables and stir them into the sauce; if you'd like to add snap peas, wait until the last 2 minutes of cooking time before adding them. Snow peas will cook in about 1 minute.

Trout with Pumpkin Seed Sage Butter

Yield: 2 servings

It's easy to debone a trout, especially after you've done it a couple of times. Once cooked and plated, with a fork, peel back the meat from the top thick end of the backbone. Work towards the tail a little at a time and keep the fillet intact with the help of a soup spoon held upside down on the skin side of the fillet. Once the top fillet is resting on the plate, loosen the backbone with the fork going underneath it at the thick end of the bottom fillet. With the bone between the fork on the bottom and the spoon on the top, gently pull the bone up and remove it. Remove any stray little bones you see. Roll back the top fillet to regain its "whole" look.

INGREDIENTS

10-12 oz. trout, bone-in, head off, cut in half crosswise | 1
Sea salt | 3/4 tsp.
Black pepper | 1/4 tsp.
Fine cornmeal | 1/2 cup
Extra virgin olive oil | 1 tsp.
Dried sage | 1 tsp.
Butter | 2 tsp.
Pumpkin seeds | 3 Tbsp.
Juice from fresh lemon and cider vinegar | 2 Tbsp. each
Baby greens | 1 cup

DIRECTIONS

On a plate, mix 1/2 tsp. each of salt and sage, the pepper, and the cornmeal. Coat trout with this mixture; shake off excess. Melt 1 tsp. each of olive oil and butter in a medium skillet. Add fish, cover pan, and cook over medium heat for 4 minutes (don't cover if using boneless trout). Uncover, cook 4-1/2 minutes longer, turn over with a spatula, and cook for 4-6 minutes, or until done (fish will peel away with a fork at the thicker end of the backbone). Plate fish on the baby greens. To the same pan, melt the remaining 1 tsp. butter. Add pumpkin seeds and the remaining 1/2 tsp. sage. Stir for 1 minute until butter is lightly browned. Add lemon, vinegar, and the remaining 1/4 tsp. salt. Pour over fish and greens.

VARIATIONS

To help retain moisture if using boneless trout, stuff 1 cup of fresh baby spinach (instead of lining the plates with baby greens) between the fillets. Sprinkle with salt and close; cook uncovered over medium heat, as directed above, for 6-7 minutes on each side, or until done. If some spinach falls out during this process, just stuff it back in; as the spinach wilts, it will hold in place.

This dish is also delicious when prepared with cod fillets in place of the trout. Adjust cooking time to approximately 10 minutes per inch of thickness.

Lemon Mushroom Chicken
Yield: 3 servings

INGREDIENTS

White wine or chicken broth | 1/3 cup

Sea salt | 1/2 tsp. plus additional 1/2 tsp.

Ground black pepper | 1/4 tsp.

Garlic cloves, crushed and peeled | 3

Lemon, juiced | 1 (2 Tbsp. of juice)

Mushrooms, sliced | 8-9

Large chicken drumsticks, or small thighs *see variations | 3

Snap peas | 1-1/2 cups

Mustard greens, swiss chard, or kale, chopped | 3 cups

Dijon mustard and capers | 1 Tbsp. each

Cold butter | 2-1/2 tsp.

Baby spinach | 2-3 handfuls

Hot cooked rice | 3 cups (1 cup raw)

DIRECTIONS

Combine white wine or broth, black pepper, garlic, and mushrooms in the bottom of a medium saucepan. Top with the chicken and sprinkle all with 2 Tbsp. lemon juice and 1/2 tsp. salt. Bring to a boil, lower heat, cover, and simmer gently for 25-30 minutes, or until chicken is just cooked through. Turn chicken over, add the capers and snap peas; bring back to a simmer, cover, and continue cooking for 1-2 minutes. Stir in leafy greens and remaining salt, cover, and simmer gently for 1-1/2 minutes longer, or until vegetables are cooked al dente. Meanwhile, while the vegetables are cooking, divide hot rice onto the middle of each plate. Spread rice out, making a well in the center. Add spinach to the well, and top spinach with the meats and greens when done. Whisk Dijon into the simmering liquid, and boil to reduce the sauce, approximately 1 minute. Meanwhile, remove the skin from the chicken. Stir butter into the sauce until blended through and pour it over the chicken and vegetables.

VARIATIONS

*Substitute 2 bone-in chicken breast halves, halved again crosswise, for the drumsticks; you'll have an extra piece to freeze or cook for leftovers. If the breast halves are small, use 3, and leave them "whole." Adjust cooking time, as necessary.

*For **Lemon Chicken and Prawns** and a more quickly prepared meal, you can substitute the bone-in chicken parts with a combination of prawns and sliced boneless chicken breast tenders, or either-or. Have all the ingredients ready; the chicken will cook through within approximately 6-9 minutes, depending on their size; the prawns about 4-6 minutes, depending on their size and whether they're peeled or not. Meanwhile, continue as directed above.

White Bean and Sausage Stew

Yield: 4 servings

INGREDIENTS

Dried great northern or cannellini beans | 2 cups

Extra virgin olive oil and butter | 1 tsp. each

Large onion, 1/4" dice | 1

Sea salt | 1/2 tsp. plus additional 1-1/2 tsp.

Sage, chile flakes, and thyme | 1 tsp. each

Garlic cloves, minced | 4

Canned whole tomatoes in juice | 1 – 28 oz. can

Bay leaf | 1

Fresh Italian sausage links (if using hot, omit chiles) | 3/4-1 lb.

Chard or mustard greens, de-stemmed and chopped | 1 bunch

Lemon juice | 1/2 tsp.

Grated Romano cheese | 1/2 cup

DIRECTIONS

Two or more hours earlier, in a large pot, cook beans, partially covered, by simmering them in water 2" above their level (replenishing water, as needed, raising heat to bring back to a simmer, and lowering heat back to keep it at a gentle simmer) for 1-1/4 - 1-1/2 hours. Add 1/2 tsp. of salt and black pepper to taste, and cook, uncovered, 15-20 minutes longer, or until just tender and most of the liquid has evaporated.

Meanwhile, poke holes all around each sausage link. Fit into the bottom of a small-medium saucepan. Almost cover with water and bring to a boil. Lower heat and simmer for 10 minutes, turning over once (this will drain off excess fat in the sausage). Rinse sausage and set aside. Warm the oil and butter in a medium saucepan; sauté the onion, 1/2 tsp. salt, and the spices over medium heat for 2 minutes. Stir in the garlic and cook for 1 minute. Add tomatoes and the remaining tsp. of salt. Rinse the tomato can one-third to halfway full with water and add to the pot. Cut the partially cooled sausage into 1-1/4" slices and add along with the cooked beans and the small amount of liquid remaining with them. Bring to a boil, lower heat, and simmer, partially covered, for 30 minutes. Stir in greens and lemon; cook 2 minutes longer. Serve with grated cheese and a tossed green salad.

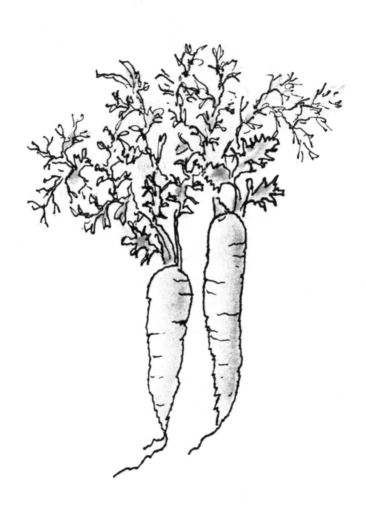

CHAPTER 9

Flavorful and nutritious "food desert" recipes; low- and no-cook meals and snacks

Many people in this country have little or no access to fresh nutritious food; their neighborhoods contain inadequate supermarkets or none at all. In many cases, highly-processed foods, usually more affordable and available than fresh whole foods, provide the calories people need to sustain their energy and keep their stomachs full, but not the nutritional value to promote good health. These conditions are exacerbated by a policy inclusion encouraged by the sugar industry and food processing giants, and set by the government, that allows "junk food" to be purchased with food stamps. You cannot use them to buy a hot whole roasted chicken, but you can buy highly processed frozen dinners, high sodium shelf-stable foods, sweets, bakery items, sweetened beverages, candy, desserts, and high in fat, salty snacks. Now called SNAP, this important, and for the most part, successful program helps many low-income families put healthy food on their tables, and the need for it has been magnified by the coronavirus pandemic. However, SNAP would be more beneficial to its recipients, and fairer to all taxpayers, if it limited accepted purchases to mostly fresh, frozen, and shelf-stable fruits, vegetables, legumes, whole grains, dairy, and eggs, with limited, but ample, allowances for meat, poultry, and fish. Concurrently, we must make those foods available to recipients, and allocated benefits would need to reflect the often higher costs for the healthier foods. SNAP dollars, presently accepted at a majority of farmer's markets, should be accepted at all of them.

Although many organizations and local residents dedicate themselves to the goal of increasing access to quality food, often they survive on temporary grants and volunteers, which undermine their effectiveness. We can increase their influence and productivity by making available to them many of the subsidies now given to factory farms and largely automated agribusinesses, instead, funding projects that promote organic urban and suburban agriculture and greenhouse food production across our nation. We already have systems in place that produce high yields in small spaces, and bringing low- and middle-income residents closer to healthy food sources is very much in our national security interest. Presently, however, there exist few wholesome food options in most inner-city neighborhoods, as well as in many of our small rural towns.

I have visited convenience stores and dollar stores that serve low-income communities to research the foods typically available, yet I've never lived in a food desert. My parents, throughout many of their child-rearing years, often struggled to make ends meet. There were times when my "stay at home" mom would find temporary jobs to help see us through those rougher patches; however, they were always able to provide us with ample amounts of fresh nutritious food. I suspect that was an easier task in the era before processed and fast foods became commonplace. As a child, I remember mom saying to me, "You'll never starve as long as you have canned tuna in your cupboard." In those days tuna cost a lot less than today, although it remains an economical food. Whenever tuna went on sale (eight cans for a dollar!) my mother, and my grandparents, would buy plenty. It wasn't uncommon to show up visiting one another with gifts of canned tuna; in that way, we were able to take advantage of sales that ran at different times in three New York City boroughs (perhaps this represents my first experience with cooperative purchasing). I can still clearly see the smiling faces of my grandparents holding the cans they brought for us as I opened our front door to greet them. I guess you could call having "a cupboard stocked with tuna" our mantra in a family that lived through the Great Depression. Yet I never had to experience such privation. As luck would have it, my only encounter with food "want" occurred when given the code FHB - Family Hold Back - whenever we had unexpected guests drop in at mealtime.

As an adult, my career in the food business allowed me to eat many meals at work. With a growing school-aged son, my partner and I enjoyed the benefits of purchasing our food (and wine) at wholesale prices throughout the five years we owned our restaurant; this represented one of the few perks of working eighty hours a week. At other times, however, I struggled to have enough good food in the house for my son. My paycheck-to-paycheck existence and typical sixty-plus hour workweek forced me to buy cheap, easy to prepare processed foods like Top Ramen (10 packs for a dollar). I taught Danny to always prepare the soup with as many added vegetables as he could, and I believe that for the most part, he did (having walked in on him many times while he enjoyed a bowl). I've also spent the bulk of my adult years living in New York City and California, a city and a state where, in my experience, fresh produce was readily available. I've been fortunate in so many ways, and my gratitude for what I have increases as I see a much larger disparity now between those with the opportunities and means to adequately support themselves and their families, and those without these opportunities.

I hope that the following recipes can help those who currently live the food desert reality. I encourage creative substitutions for those ingredients neither available nor enjoyed.

Even when not living in a food desert, some people lack a functional kitchen, including a great number of students. And many people from all walks of life have extremely limited time and energy to cook, the case for many working parents. The first group of recipes will focus on low-product access and affordability, the last group on low- and no-cook meals and snacks; recipes in the middle occupy both categories.

Linguine with Canned Tuna and Tomatoes
Yield: 3 servings

INGREDIENTS

Olive or other cooking oil | 1-1/2 tsp.

Small onion, chopped 1/4" dice | 1

Salt | 1-1/4 tsp.

Crushed red chiles or Tabasco | 1/2 tsp.

Thyme and oregano | 1/2 tsp. ea. (or 1 tsp. Italian seasoning)

Black pepper | 1/8 tsp.

Small green bell pepper, chopped, 1/4" dice | 1

Whole tomatoes, in juice| 1–28 oz. can (or 2 – 15 oz. cans)

Canned tuna, drained | 2

Black (preferably Kalamata) olives, pitted, chopped or sliced | 16-18

Capers (or pepperoncini, chopped) | 1/4 cup

Lemon juice | 1-1/2 Tbsp.

Pasta water | approximately 1/4 cup

Butter | approximately 1 Tbsp.

Frozen ch. spinach, thawed | 1 (10-12 oz) package

Pasta of choice | 1/2 lb.

DIRECTIONS

Break up the frozen spinach a bit and let it thaw in the colander that you'll use to drain the pasta. In a large pot, bring a generous amount of water to a boil. In a medium saucepan, warm oil and sauté the onion over medium-low heat for 3 minutes. Stir in 1/2 tsp. salt, the chiles, thyme, and oregano. Cook for 2 minutes. Meanwhile, pour the tomatoes into a bowl and crush them thoroughly with your hand. Add them to the pan with the tomato juice, bell pepper, lemon juice, black pepper, and the remaining 3/4 tsp. salt. Stir well and simmer, partially covered, for 5 minutes. Stir in tuna, capers, and olives. Simmer slowly, partially covered, for 8–12 minutes while you cook the pasta in well-salted water until al dente. Reserving 1/3 cup of liquid in case you need to thin the sauce at the end, drain the pasta over the spinach. Adjust the consistency of the sauce, if desired, and while simmering, stir in 2-3 tsp. of the butter until it's blended through. Add the pasta, and gently mix to combine. Serve hot.

Vegetable Frittata with Spam
Yield: 6 servings

Spam contains too much sodium per serving to label it a healthy food. If fresh smoked ham (not typically as high in sodium) is available, I would use that instead. There are a total of three recipes in this chapter that list Spam as an ingredient. I used only one can for all three dishes. As my dad would say, "if it's used in moderation, it's probably O.K."

INGREDIENTS

Onion, and poblano or green bell pepper 1/4" dice | 1/2 cup each

Spam or ham, finely chopped | 2/3 cup

Small russet potato, 1/4" dice | 1

Cooking oil | 2 tsp.

Salt | 3/4 tsp.

Black pepper | 1/8 tsp.

Thyme (or Italian seasoning) | 1/4 tsp.

Water | 1/4 cup (use spinach water, if it's ready to be squeezed dry)

Frozen ch. spinach | 1 – 10-12 oz. package, thawed and squeezed dry

Eggs, room temperature | 6

Milk | 2/3 cup

Cayenne or Tabasco sauce | 1/8 - 1/4 tsp., to taste

Swiss, or other cheese, grated or crumbled | 2/3 – 3/4 cup

DIRECTIONS

Warm oil in a medium-sized skillet; sauté onion, spam, potato, 1/2 tsp. salt, and the black pepper over medium heat for 5 minutes. Stir in poblano, add the water, cover, and steam over low heat for 10-12 minutes, or until potatoes are just done. Simmer, uncovered, until water evaporates. Stir in the squeezed dry spinach and remove from heat. Meanwhile, in a medium bowl, whisk the eggs, milk, and hot pepper until well mixed and frothy; stir in the cheese. Being careful that the eggs don't curdle, slowly pour into the slightly cooled vegetable mixture, stirring well to blend. Spoon into a greased 9" pie pan or 9" square baking pan. Bake in a pre-heated 375-degree oven for approximately 35-40 minutes, or until just set in the center. Let cool 5-10 minutes before cutting.

VARIATIONS

Replace meat and/or potato with a similar amount of sliced shiitakes and additional onion and pepper.

For egg bites, spoon the egg mixture into a greased muffin tin. Bake in a preheated 375-degree oven for approximately 20 minutes, or until just set in the center.

Salmon Cakes with Tzatziki Sauce
Yield: 2 - 3 servings

INGREDIENTS

Canned salmon | 1 – 6-8 oz. can
Pinto beans, rinsed and drained well | 1 - 15 oz. can
Whole wheat bread, chopped fine | 1 small slice (1/3 cup)
Scallions, thinly sliced on diagonal (or chopped parsley) | 1/3 cup
Red or green bell pepper, 1/4" dice | 1/3 cup
Salt and cayenne pepper | 1/2 tsp. each
Lemon | 1 (2/3 for 1-1/2 Tbsp. of juice and 1/3 for wedges)
Egg, beaten | 1
Olive or other cooking oil | 1-1/2 tsp.
Lettuce or spinach, torn into bite-sized pieces | 2 – 3 large handfuls
Frozen peas, thawed or fresh snap peas, halved diagonally | 1/2 – 3/4 cup
Avocado (optional) | 1
Cornmeal for dredging (optional) | 2/3 cup

DIRECTIONS

Prepare tzatziki sauce (recipe below); set aside at room temperature. Drain salmon well. If packed in its own juice, stir liquid into salmon and then drain. In a medium-large bowl, mash 1 cup of the pinto beans well. Reserve the rest for the salad. Add the vegetables, salmon, seasonings, lemon, egg, and bread; combine gently, but thoroughly. Shape into 4 oblong patties (not too thin), or 3 larger ones for 3 servings. Spread the cornmeal onto a plate, if using. Lightly coat the tops and bottoms (not the sides) of the patties and pat off the excess. Gently place them in the warmed oil in a medium-large skillet. Brown over medium-high heat for approximately 3-1/2 minutes on each side. Meanwhile, toss greens, remaining beans, and peas or snap peas together on each plate. Cut remaining lemon into 2-3 wedges for plate garnish. Top greens with the patties, drizzle with tzatziki; serve remaining sauce on the side. Serve overlapping slices of avocado, if desired, on the plates alongside the salmon cakes; sprinkle avocado with a little lemon and salt.

VARIATION

For **Oyster Cakes**: If you live in an area where fresh, jarred, or canned (but not smoked) oysters are available, use 3/4 – 1 cup of drained, chopped, and drained again (save the liquid, if desired*) oyster meat in place of the salmon; increase bread crumbs by about 1/4 cup, only if necessary, to hold the mixture together. With those changes, follow the above recipe.

*If the oyster liquid is free of chemical preservatives, mix with milk (1-1/2 - 1 ratio), a touch of white wine, and a bit of salt and cayenne; simmer for 2-3 minutes.

Tzatziki Sauce

Yield: 2 - 3 servings

INGREDIENTS

Plain yogurt | 1-1/3 cups
Garlic cloves, minced | 2
Olive, or other cooking oil | 2 tsp.
*Fresh dill, mint, and/or parsley | 1/4 cup (or 1 Tbsp. dried) total
Salt | 1/4 tsp. plus additional 1/2 tsp.
Cucumber, grated | 1/2 (approximately 2/3 – 3/4 cup)
Juice from fresh lemon | 1 (2 Tbsp.)

DIRECTIONS

Grate, or finely chop, the cucumber. Place in a small bowl and sprinkle with 1/4 tsp. salt; let sit for 5–10 minutes. Squeeze cucumber of excess moisture. Add to a serving bowl along with the remaining ingredients. Mix well, let sit 15 minutes, or longer, for flavors to blend.

Note: Although using fresh chopped cilantro in place of the dill, mint, or parsley, isn't traditional, it would make a flavorful substitution.

Not Quite Grandma's Split Pea Soup
Yield: 6 - 8 servings

My grandma, Ida, used beef marrow bones, not Spam or ham, to prepare this delicious soup. That represents the healthiest version, although it remains a nutritious soup however you prepare it. If you do use the beef bones, make sure you remove, chop up, and add all of the marrow to the soup before adding the grated carrot and egg.

INGREDIENTS

Dried green split peas | 1 lb.
Water | 8 cups
Carrots, 1 broken in half, 2 grated | 3
Celery stalk, broken in half | 1
Small onion, cut in half | 1
Parsley | 5 sprigs
Garlic cloves, finely chopped | 3
Salt | 1-1/4 tsp.
Black pepper and thyme| 1/4 tsp. each
Spam or smoked ham, finely chopped | 3/4 cup
Bay leaf | 1
Eggs, partially beaten in bowl | 2

DIRECTIONS

Combine all ingredients except for the grated carrots and eggs. Bring to a boil, stirring occasionally. Reduce the heat to medium-low; simmer approximately 1-1/4 hrs. or until split peas are tender and breaking down. Remove onion, carrot, celery, and parsley. Sprinkle in grated carrot and simmer for 5 minutes. To make the egg drops, stir the soup while slowly adding the "not quite thoroughly" beaten egg. Turn heat off and serve hot.

RECIPES

Linguine with Red Clam Sauce
Yield: 3 servings

Similar to the Seafood Pasta in the previous chapter, this recipe utilizes more readily available canned clams. If only whole canned clams are available, roughly chop them before adding to the sauce.

INGREDIENTS

Olive or other cooking oil | 1-1/2 tsp.
Onion, 1/2" dice | 1/2
Garlic, chopped | 2 cloves
Salt | 3/4 tsp.
Thyme and oregano | 1/2 tsp. each (or 1 tsp. Italian seasoning)
Crushed red chiles or Tabasco | 1/2 tsp.
White wine | 1/2 cup
Diced tomatoes in juice | 1-15 oz. can (approx. 1-1/2 c.)
Salt | 1/2 tsp.
Chopped clams in juice | 2 - 6.5 oz. cans
Lemon juice | 1 Tbsp. plus 1 tsp. (approximately 2/3 of a lemon)
Frozen chopped spinach | 10-12 oz. package
Cold butter | 1 Tbsp.
Linguine (or spaghetti), cooked al dente in salted water | 1/2 lb.

DIRECTIONS

Let spinach thaw in a colander in your sink, breaking it apart periodically. Bring a large pot of water to a boil. Meanwhile, in a medium-large skillet or saucepan over medium heat, sauté the onion in oil for 3 minutes, stir in garlic and spices, and cook for 1 minute longer. Careful not to burn the garlic, turn heat to medium-high, wait 15 seconds, and add wine. Shake the pan, and after another 15 seconds, turn heat to medium-low; let simmer 1-1/2 minutes. Stir in tomato, and simmer, partially covered, for 8 minutes. Meanwhile, generously salt the boiling water and add the pasta. After the sauce has simmered for 8 minutes, add only the clam juice to the sauce, and boil, uncovered, for 2-1/2 minutes. Bring the heat down to low and cover the pan. When pasta is just al dente, drain it over the spinach (reserving 1/3 cup of the water, if needed for thinning the sauce). Stir the clams and lemon juice into the sauce. Cook over medium heat for 35-40 seconds, add the butter, and stir until thoroughly blended in. Shut the fire, add pasta, combine well, and adjust seasoning and consistency, if needed; plate immediately.

Note: If canned tomatoes in puree are all that's available, rinse the empty can with 1/4 - 1/3 cup of water and add it to the pot.

Sautéed Cabbage with Onion and Potatoes

Yield: 2 servings

INGREDIENTS

Onion, 1/2" dice | 1 small

Spam, ham, or prosciutto, finely
    chopped | 1/2 cup

Cooking oil | 1-1/2 tsp.

Salt | 1/4 tsp. plus additional 1/4 tsp.

Black pepper | 1/8 tsp.

Small new potatoes, halved | 8

Green cabbage, shredded | 1/2

DIRECTIONS

Place potatoes in a medium saucepan. Barely cover them with water. Bring to a boil, add 1/4 tsp. salt, and cover with lid slightly askew to allow some steam to escape. Simmer slowly, 15-20 minutes, or until cooked through but firm; drain. Sauté onion and spam in hot oil over medium heat until meat is crispy. Stir in cabbage, salt, and pepper, and cook approximately 2-1/2 minutes. The cabbage should be somewhat wilted but al dente. Mix in potatoes and serve hot.

Pasta with Fresh Sausage and Peas
Yield: 3 servings

INGREDIENTS

Oregano, thyme, and sage | 1/2 tsp. each (or 1-1/2 tsp. Italian seasoning)

Fennel seed (optional) and red chile flakes | 1/2 tsp. each

Salt | 1/2 tsp. plus an additional 1/2 tsp.

Ground meat of your choice | 1/2 lb.

Olive or other cooking oil | 1-1/2 tsp.

Small onion and green bell, 1/2" dice | 1 each

Garlic cloves, chopped | 3

Dry sherry or apple juice (or a mix) | 1/2 cup

Pasta water | 1/3 cup

Lemon juice and butter | 2 tsp. each

Peas, frozen or fresh | 3/4 cup

Spinach | 1 bunch fresh, or 2/3 of a 12 oz. package, frozen

Pasta (I prefer linguine with this dish)| 1/2 lb.

Grated Parmesan cheese | enough to top each serving

DIRECTIONS

Bring a generous amount of salted water to a boil for the pasta. Place spinach and peas in a colander in the sink. In a bowl, combine ground meat with 1/2 tsp. salt and the other seasonings; mix well. In a large skillet, warm oil and sauté onion with the remaining 1/2 tsp. of salt over medium heat for 4 minutes. Add garlic, and cook 1 minute; add the sausage mix, mashing it with the back of a spoon to separate, until just cooked through. Pour, or blot, off excess grease. Stir in bell pepper, turn up the heat, wait 20 seconds, and with the overhead fan on, add the sherry. Tip pan to set sherry aflame and simmer on low heat for 1 minute (if you're using sherry and have no overhead fan, omit this step and simmer for 2 minutes longer). Partially cover the skillet and turn off the heat while the pasta cooks; 2 minutes before the pasta is al dente, turn the heat back on under the sauce to medium-high. When simmering again, add 1/4 cup of pasta water and lemon juice, and stir well for 20 seconds. Raise heat, stir in butter, and when blended through and sauce thickens, turn off the heat. Drain the pasta well in the colander over the peas and greens and mix thoroughly with the sauce. Top with cheese, and serve immediately.

Turmeric Cauliflower, Potatoes & Chickpeas

Yield: 4 servings

INGREDIENTS

Cauliflower, cut into large florets | 1 small head
Medium new potatoes, quartered | 8
Chickpeas | 1–15 oz. can
Salt | 1 tsp.
Ground black or cayenne pepper | 1/4 tsp.
Cumin seed (optional) | 1-1/4 tsp.
Turmeric (or *curry powder) | 2-1/2 tsp.
Olive or other cooking oil | 1 Tbsp.
Lemon juice | 2 Tbsp.
Rice | 2 cups
Small onion, diced and browned slowly in the 2 tsp. of butter | 1
Butter | 2 tsp.

DIRECTIONS

In a small saucepan (one with a lid), slowly brown the onion in the butter; this will take roughly 12 minutes. Stir in (1 cup each brown and white Basmati) rice and 2-3/4 cups of water. Bring to a boil and let simmer, covered, over low heat for 25 minutes; let sit for 10 (or use another variety of rice and follow package directions). Meanwhile, in a medium saucepan, add potatoes and water to barely cover them. Add 1/4 tsp. salt, bring to a boil and simmer, partially covered, until just tender but not falling apart, approximately 18 minutes. Drain potatoes, reserving 3/4 cup of the liquid. Rinse and dry the same pan, add cumin seed, and lightly toast over medium-low heat until fragrant; then return reserved liquid to the pan; stir in turmeric, remaining 1/2 tsp. salt, pepper, lemon juice, and oil. Bring the liquid to a simmer, stir in cauliflower and chickpeas, and bring back to a simmer. Cover, and let steam over medium heat for 4 minutes. Stir in the potatoes, cover, and cook 1 more minute, or until cauliflower is al dente; serve on plates alongside the caramelized onion rice.

*Omit cumin seed if you use curry powder instead of turmeric.

VARIATION

If you want a complete protein meal without the rice, add an additional 1/4 tsp. of cayenne (optional) to the reserved potato water. When vegetables are done, top each serving with tzatziki (see recipe index) or serve the dish with **Lassi**, an Indian yogurt drink made by pureeing fruit with sweetener and yogurt in a blender, and serving it well chilled. My favorite combines 3 c. plain (not Greek) yogurt, 1-1/2 cups cold water, 3 Tbsp. of honey, 1/8 t. salt, and the flesh from 2-3 mangos (2-1/4 - 2-1/2 cups of fresh or frozen pulp).

Chicken Livers with Dried Apricots
Yield: 2 servings

INGREDIENTS

Olive or other cooking oil | 1-1/2 tsp.

Thyme and black pepper | 1/4 tsp. each

Salt | 1/2 tsp.

Onion, 1/4" dice | 2/3 cup

Dried apricots, 1/4" dice | 1/3 cup

Hot water | 3/4 cup

Chicken livers, cleaned and dried | 1/2 lb.

Apricot soaking liquid and white wine | 1/3 cup each

Balsamic (or other) vinegar | 2 tsp.

Cold butter | 1-1/2 tsp.

DIRECTIONS

Soak apricots in 3/4 cup of hot water. Allow to sit while preparing the other ingredients. Warm oil in a medium-large skillet; sauté onion over medium heat for 4 minutes. Stir in livers, salt, pepper, and thyme. Cook for approximately 4 minutes. When browned, add apricots; increase the heat to medium-high, turn livers, wait 45 seconds, and add the wine. Shake the pan, lower heat to medium-low, and simmer for 1-1/2 minutes; add the soaking liquid and balsamic; stir well to incorporate the bits from the bottom of the pan. Cook over medium-low heat, partially covered, for 2-3 minutes, or until the livers are cooked, but still pink in the center. Add butter, stir until blended through, and remove from heat. A tossed green salad, with canned beans added, goes well with this dish.

VARIATIONS

Use 3/4 cup of fresh chopped pear or apple in place of the apricots. Allow them to sit barely covered in hot water, so you'll have 1/3 cup of soaking liquid for the sauce.

You can use other chicken parts, or pork chops, in place of the livers. After deglazing the pan with the wine and soaking liquid, bring to a simmer, turn the heat down to low, cover, and finish cooking the meat.

For **Chicken Livers Marsala**, bring a pot of water to a boil to cook pasta (I prefer long noodles, like linguine or fettuccine, for this dish). Omit the apricots and proceed as directed above. Substitute Marsala wine for the soaking liquid. With your overhead fan on, add it just before you add the white wine. Tip the pan a little bit and try to get it to flame up. It's O.K. if it doesn't. The alcohol will cook out whether you get a flame or not; lower the heat, take a minute or two to deglaze the pan, and remove it from the heat. Decrease the vinegar to 1 tsp., and add; cover the pan. When pasta is almost al dente, uncover the sauce and bring it back to a simmer. Add some pasta water if the sauce has reduced too much; then drain the pasta well. Increase the butter to 2 tsp. and stir it into the simmering sauce until blended through; combine pasta with the sauce and chicken livers, and serve with grated Parmesan or Romano cheese.

RECIPES

Canned Mackerel with Vegetables and Rice
Yield: 2-3 servings

INGREDIENTS

Olive, sesame, or other cooking oil | 1-1/4 tsp.

Salt | 1/4 tsp. plus additional 1/4 tsp. for the rice

Ground black pepper and crushed red chile pepper | 1/4 tsp. each

Bok choy or green cabbage, 1 - 1-1/4" wedges | 4

*Mackerel, drained | 1-15 oz. can

Soy sauce and water | 1/4 cup each

Lemon or lime juice (or vinegar) | 2 Tbsp.

Snow or snap peas or bean sprouts (optional) | 1-1/4 cups

Butter | 1 tsp. plus an additional 1/2 tsp. for the rice

Roughly chopped cilantro (optional) | 1/3 cup
Hot cooked rice | 2-1/4 – 3 cups (3/4 - 1 cup raw)

DIRECTIONS

Over medium heat, sauté bok choy or cabbage in the oil; sprinkle with 1/4 tsp. salt and cook, turning vegetables once, for 5-6 minutes. Add mackerel, careful not to break up the big pieces. Add soy sauce, water, peppers, and lemon. Shake the pan and cook over medium heat, uncovered, for 1 minute. Gently turn over the fish and vegetables; add snap peas, if using. Cover the pan and cook for one minute longer. If using snow peas or bean sprouts, add them now, cover, and cook 30-45 seconds longer. Plate the mackerel and vegetables, leaving as much of the sauce in the pan as you can. Bring back to a simmer and stir 1 tsp. butter into the sauce until blended through; pour over the fish and vegetables. Stir cilantro (if using), and remaining butter and salt into the hot rice; add to the plate. Alternatively, serve as a "rice bowl" meal.

*King Mackerel (especially from the Pacific) can have high mercury content. If that's all that's available to you, consider choosing another canned fish for this dish, like sardines, solid-packed tuna, or whole clams. If you substitute whole clams, use 1/4 cup of their juices in place of the water and add the clams to the pan during the last minute of cooking time; they will get tough if overheated.

VARIATIONS

Substitute broccoli, cut into large 2-1/2" florets with 2" stems, or whole (halved, if large) Brussels sprouts for the bok choy or cabbage.

This is a versatile recipe. If you have garlic and fresh ginger on hand, you can chop a tablespoon of each and add them to the pan 3-4 minutes after you've begun to sauté the vegetables. You can also add 1 - 1-1/2 tsp. honey with the soy and water, if desired.

Instead of using mackerel, add fresh shellfish, like clams, mussels, and/or oysters as soon as you turn the vegetables for the first time. Cover the pan, raise the heat to medium-high, shake the pan to settle the seafood, and cook for 2 minutes. Uncover and add 3 Tbsp. of white wine in place of the quarter cup of water. Add the soy, black and chile peppers, and lemon (add prawns, if desired); bring to a simmer and cover the pan. After 2 minutes, uncover, and begin to remove the mollusks from the pan as soon as their shells pop open; remove prawns when just cooked through. Remove the vegetables as soon as they're cooked al dente. Meanwhile, lower the heat if the sauce is reducing too quickly. Throw away any mollusks that don't open. Stir the butter into the sauce until blended through; pour over the shellfish and plate alongside the vegetables and rice or pour the sauce over a small bed of vermicelli noodles with the seafood and vegetables surrounding them.

Harold's Bean Stew
Yield: 8 servings

INGREDIENTS

Onion, chopped | 1
Cooking oil | 2 tsp.
Cumin and coriander | 1-1/4 tsp. each
Turmeric (paprika or annatto)| 1-1/4 tsp.
Crushed red chile flakes | 3/4 tsp.
Ground black pepper | 1/2 tsp.
Beans, assorted | 4-15 oz. cans
Tomatoes, diced in juice | 2 - 14.5 (or 1 - 28) oz. cans
Water | two empty 14-15 oz. canfuls
Salt | 1 Tbsp.
Tabasco sauce | 3/4 tsp. or to taste
Frozen peas and frozen corn | 2/3 - 3/4 cups each
Chopped mustard greens, kale or *collards | 3 cups (optional)
Lemon juice | 2 tsp. (optional)

DIRECTIONS

Over medium-low heat, sauté onion, spices, and 1 tsp. of salt in the oil for 2-3 minutes. Stir in beans, tomatoes, 2 canfuls of water, the remaining 2 tsp. of salt, and Tabasco. Bring to a simmer and cook for 12-15 minutes. Stir in peas, corn (and greens, if using). Bring back to a simmer and cook for 1-2 minutes longer. Stir in lemon juice, if desired.

*If using collards, add them to the pot after the beans and tomatoes have cooked for 10 minutes; then proceed as above.

VARIATION

For a complete protein meal, add cooked rice to the bowl, or top stew with grated cheese.

Spinach and Cheese Omelette

Yield: 2 Omelettes

The result to strive for when making an omelette is one that's thin and moist (not runny), and not puffy and dry. It could be very slightly browned, but preferably not brown at all. It may take practice, but if you have a good egg pan, you will be successful. You can alternatively make this a scrambled egg dish, but be careful not to overcook the eggs.

INGREDIENTS

Frozen chopped spinach, thawed, and squeezed dry | 2 cups
Eggs | 4
Salt | 1/4 tsp.
Cayenne or ground black pepper | 1/8 tsp.
Milk or water | 2 Tbsp.
Cheese of your choice, grated or crumbled | 1/2 cup
Butter | 1 tsp.

DIRECTIONS

Thaw spinach and grate the cheese. Combine eggs, salt, pepper, and milk or water in a bowl. Whisk, or stir vigorously with a fork, from the bottom-up, lifting the fork as you beat to aerate the eggs. Squeeze the spinach dry, and stir into the egg mixture. Make one omelet at a time in an 8" seasoned pan or both together in one 12" skillet (or two 8" egg pans). Melt 1/2 tsp. butter per omelet over medium-high heat. When the pan is very hot and butter is melted and bubbly, add half the egg mixture per person. Allow eggs to begin to set on the bottom of the pan (this will take approximately 15 seconds), and quickly stir with a wooden spoon 3-4 times. Turn heat off immediately. Push the set egg from the outer edge of the pan slightly towards the center and tilt the pan to allow the runny uncooked egg to hit the bottom of the hot pan; continue doing this until most of the runny egg has dried and set; sprinkle egg with the cheese. Fold half the omelet over onto itself and cover the pan. Put the burner on the lowest setting for 45 seconds to one minute only, then turn off the heat, leaving the pan there until cheese is melted and eggs are just cooked through, about 45 seconds to one minute longer. During this last step, if the bottom begins to brown and the cheese is not yet melted, flip the omelette over on its other side, and re-cover the pan to finish. The burner should still be hot without needing to turn it on, but turn on to its lowest setting, if necessary. When done, slide onto a plate; if you used one 12" pan, cut the omelette in half crosswise with a spatula and plate. Serve with a small baked potato or toast, and lightly salted sliced tomato for a full meal.

Coconut Milk Pumpkin Soup
Yield: 4 - 6 servings

INGREDIENTS

Olive, or other cooking oil, or butter | 2 tsp.

Onion, 1/4" dice | 1

Garlic cloves, finely chopped | 4

Salt | 1-3/4 tsp.

Black pepper and cayenne | 1/4 tsp. each

Thyme | 1/2 tsp.

Curry powder | 2 tsp.

Water | 1/2 cup

Pumpkin puree | 2–15 oz. cans

Chicken broth (or water) | 1–15 oz. can (or just under 2 cups)

Unsweetened coconut milk, preferably lite* | 1–15 oz. can

Pumpkin seeds, toasted in dry pan | 3 Tbsp.

Chopped fresh basil, cilantro, or parsley | 2 Tbsp.

DIRECTIONS

Warm oil and sauté onion over medium heat for 4 minutes. Stir in garlic and spices, and cook over medium-low heat for 2 minutes. Whisk in 1/2 cup of water, pumpkin, broth or water, and milk. Bring to a boil and simmer slowly, covered, for 18 minutes, and uncovered for 2-3 minutes longer. Mix herb and pumpkin seeds to garnish each serving.

*Look for lite coconut milk with only coconut milk and water (perhaps guar gum, as well) on the ingredient list, and nothing else.

Quick Bean and Cabbage Stew
Yield: 2-3 servings

INGREDIENTS

Olive, or other cooking oil | 2 tsp.

Onion, quartered and thinly sliced | 1

Poblano or Anahein chile, 1/4" dice | 1

Garlic cloves, finely chopped | 4

Salt | 1 tsp.

Black pepper | 1/4 tsp.

Cinnamon and nutmeg | 1/4 tsp. each

Crushed red chiles and dry mustard |
   1/2 tsp. each

Crushed canned tomatoes | 1-15 oz.
   can

Water | approximately 1-1/4 cups

Pinto, Kidney, or Northern beans,
   drained and rinsed | 1-15 oz. can

Yellow squash or zucchini, halved
   and sliced 1/3" diagonally | 1
   (approximately 2 cups)

Green cabbage, shredded | 4 cups

Chocolate, extra dark | 1/4 oz.

Butter | 2 tsp.

Queso fresco, cotija, añejo, feta, or
   Parmesan | 2-3 oz.

DIRECTIONS

Warm oil and sauté onion over medium heat, stirring occasionally, for 3 minutes. Reduce heat to medium-low, stir in 1/2 tsp. of salt, the spices, poblano, and garlic; cook for 2 minutes. Add the tomatoes and raise heat back to medium. Rinse the tomato can with water 3/4 way up, and add to the pot along with the beans and remaining salt; stir well and bring to a boil. Lower heat so that the stew simmers, covered, for 15 minutes. Raise heat to medium, stir in squash and cabbage, and cook, partially covered, for 3-4 minutes. Add chocolate and butter; stir until blended through. Serve in bowls; top with the grated or crumbled cheese. Serve with warm corn tortillas for dunking.

VARIATIONS

Serve over rice, and omit the cheese, if desired.

Add 6-8 oz. of ground meat of your choice when adding the garlic and spices to the pan. Break up ground meat with the back of a spoon to separate. If necessary, carefully pour out excess grease, or sop it up with a paper towel.

Substitute any leafy green for the cabbage.

Lemon Parmesan Rice and Peas
Yield: 2 -3 servings

INGREDIENTS

Brown and white rice (Basmati, if available) | 2/3 cup each

Salt | 1/2 tsp.

Unsalted butter | 1 tsp.

Large eggs, beaten | 2

Parmesan cheese, grated | 3/4 cup (with extra to pass around)

Lemon juice | 1/4 cup (approximately 2 lemons)

Ground black pepper | 1/4 tsp. or to taste

Parsley, chopped | 1/2 cup

Mustard greens (or other leafy green), chopped 1/2" | 1-1/3 cups

Frozen peas (or fresh, in season) | 1-1/4 cup

Sesame seeds (optional) | 1-1/4 tsp.

DIRECTIONS

Mix rice in a saucepan with 2 cups of water. Bring to a boil, cover, and set heat to low; cook for 25 minutes. Shut the fire, leaving the pan on the warm burner without removing the lid for 5-10 more minutes. Meanwhile, mix eggs, cheese, lemon juice, black pepper, parsley, greens, peas, and sesame seeds in a bowl. Stir mixture into the hot cooked rice and cook over low heat for 3-4 minutes. Serve immediately; accompany with a salad made of greens and halved grapes.

Chicken and Vegetable Curry
Yield: 6 servings

INGREDIENTS

Boneless, skinless chicken thighs, wiped dry and quartered | 5-6
Olive, or other cooking oil | 1-1/2 Tbsp.
Onion, 1/4" dice | 1 (2 cups)
Sliced shitakes or quartered crimini or white mushrooms | 4 oz.
Salt | 1 tsp. plus an additional 1-1/2 tsp.
*Coriander, cumin, and turmeric | 1-1/4 tsp. each
Cayenne pepper | 3/4 tsp.
Curry powder | 1 Tbsp.
Garlic cloves, chopped | 4 (1 Tbsp.)
Fresh ginger, minced or grated | 1-1/4 Tbsp.
Water | 2 Tbsp.

RECIPES

Dry white wine (or water) | 1/2 cup
Small-medium apples, cored and diced 1/4" | 2
Green bells, 3/4" dice | 2 (about 1 cup)
Cauliflower head, large florets | 1 (3-1/2 cups)
Crushed tomatoes | 1–15 oz. can
Plain yogurt | 1-1/4 cup
Garbanzo beans, drained and rinsed | 1–15 oz. can
Kale or Swiss chard leaves, roughly chopped | 1 bunch (6 cups)
Lemon or lime juice | 1-1/4 Tbsp.
Cooked rice | 6 cups (2 cups raw)
Fresh baby or torn spinach | 4 handfuls

DIRECTIONS

Warm oil in a large deep skillet (that has a lid) over medium heat. Sauté onion and mushrooms for 3 minutes. Moving vegetables aside, add chicken to the bottom of the pan and sprinkle with 1 tsp. salt; sear the meat until golden and turn; sprinkle with 1/2 tsp. salt. Lightly brown the other side, turn the heat down to medium-low, and stir in garlic, ginger, spices, and then 2 Tbsp. water and 1/2 tsp. salt. Stir for 1-1/2 minutes; add the wine or water, stir 1 minute to deglaze the pan; simmer for 1 minute. Stir in the tomatoes, yogurt, rinse liquid, beans, and apples. Bring to a slow simmer; cook gently, covered, for 10 minutes. Add bell pepper and cauliflower, and cook, partially covered, for 5 minutes. Uncover, stir in the greens, and cook, uncovered, for 2 minutes. Check that the chicken is cooked through and the vegetables are al dente. Stir in lemon juice and the remaining 1/2 tsp. salt, if needed. Serve over the spinach alongside the rice.

*You can use an additional 1-1/2 Tbsp. curry powder instead of the coriander, cumin, and turmeric.

VARIATION

For a meatless curry, substitute approximately 6 cups of 1" chunks of winter squash for the chicken.

Cucumber, Cauliflower & Two Bean Salad

Yield: 6 servings

INGREDIENTS

Large cucumber, partially peeled in evenly spaced long strips | 1
Cauliflower florets | from 1/2 of one head
Small red or green bell pepper, quartered, seeded, thinly sliced | 1
Scallions, thinly sliced on the bias | 2
Kidney and garbanzo beans, drained and rinsed | 1–15 oz. can each

DRESSING

Honey and water | 1/4 cup each
Apple cider vinegar | 1/2 cup
Salt | 2 tsp.

DIRECTIONS

Halve the cucumber lengthwise, remove excess seeds, and slice thinly. Sprinkle with 1/4 tsp. salt and let sit in a colander to drain while preparing the remaining vegetables. For the dressing: using warm water, mix with the honey in a large bowl; continue whisking while adding salt and vinegar. Dry cucumbers with a clean kitchen towel. Stir all the vegetables into the bowl. Let marinate at room temperature for an hour or so before serving. Transfer leftovers to a covered container and store in the refrigerator. It will last all week.

VARIATIONS

Add canned drained tuna or sardines to the salad for a quick light meal. Add some thinly shredded or chopped cabbage, if desired, or serve over baby greens.

Low- and No-Cook Snacks and Meals

The following list contains specific suggestions to create flavorful, nutritious, affordable snacks and meals that require little or no cooking.

Tuna and Cannellini Bean Salad

For 2 servings, combine 1 can of rinsed and drained cannellini or navy beans and 1 can of drained tuna, diced celery stalk, and 1/3 cup each of chopped onion, and bell pepper or tomato, 1/2 tsp. salt, 1/8 tsp. of pepper, 1 Tbsp. olive oil, and the juice of 1 fresh lemon (approximately 2 Tbsp.) Serve atop salad greens or spinach.

Peanut Butter Hummus (very little cutting required)

Make hummus using peanut butter, a staple in most kitchens, instead of tahini: mash 1 can of rinsed and drained chickpeas in a bowl with a potato masher (or food processor, if you have one). Continue mashing in 3 Tbsp. each of peanut butter and lemon juice, 1-2 cloves of finely chopped garlic, and slowly add 1/4 - 1/3 cup warm water (to make a creamy consistency), 3/4 tsp. salt, 1/8 tsp. each of black pepper, cayenne, and paprika. Mix well. Drizzle top with 1-1/2 tsp. of olive oil mixed with a 1/4 tsp. of paprika. Enjoy with vegetable sticks, rice crackers, pita, or bread of choice. If you have leftover hummus, spruce it up with additional lemon juice before serving. If you have tahini on hand, use (1/4-1/3 cup to taste) instead of peanut butter.

Avocado Dip in its Shell (very little cutting required)

For an individual serving, halve an avocado. Leave the pit attached to one half to prolong its storage life; cover and refrigerate. Leaving flesh in the other half, mash the avocado with the back of a fork. Continue mashing, adding a pinch of salt and pepper, and 1 Tbsp. of salsa if you have it on hand (or a smaller amount of hot sauce to taste). Use it as a dip right from the shell for rice crackers, bell pepper, and jicama strips. Alternatively, scoop out the avocado onto toasted bread, mash and spread with the back of a fork to cover the slice evenly; top with sliced onion, tomato, and/or bell pepper, and sprinkle with salt and pepper to taste.

Hard-boiled Egg Snack

Slice cucumber in half lengthwise, scoop out seeds, and sprinkle with a little salt. Fill the cavity with grated hard-cooked egg, pressing down on the egg, and top with radish slices; sprinkle with salt and very small amounts of black pepper and lemon juice.

Quick Baked Beans (little or no cutting required)

Pour 1 can of rinsed and drained navy beans into a small saucepan. Add 2 Tbsp. of maple syrup, 2 tsp. each of mustard (Dijon-style if you have it) and vinegar (cider vinegar if you have it), a little salt, pepper, and Tabasco. Bring to a simmer over medium-low heat; cook for 2-3 minute, and serve. I like to thinly shred cabbage and then halve the shreds crosswise, stir them into the beans after they've been simmering for a minute, and continue cooking for 1-2 minutes longer. **Variation**: lightly brown diced onion and diced Prosciutto (or other ham) in a small amount of olive oil before adding the beans to the pan.

Cottage Cheese and Pineapple Snack (little or no cutting required)

For 3-4 servings, combine 1 small can crushed or chunk pineapple in juice with 3/4 to 1 full 16 oz. container of cottage cheese. Optional additions are 1 Tbsp. each of sunflower, sesame (or flax), and pumpkin seeds, and 1/4 cup rolled oats. **Variation**: Substitute fresh-cut cantaloupe or honeydew, in season, for the canned pineapple.

Fresh Vegetable Plate

Slice a variety of raw vegetables you have on hand, like carrots, celery, radish, bell pepper, and cucumber. Sprinkle them with lime, ground chile, and salt to taste.

Alternatively, mix vegetables with a little olive oil, minced garlic, salt, pepper, and lemon juice to taste. Arrange nicely on a plate or serving dish.

❧

Chile Fruit Plate

Slice a variety of fresh fruit, like peeled and sliced melon, mango, and papaya, and pitted sliced peaches or nectarines, and whole grapes and strawberries. Sprinkle them with lime, ground chile, and a pinch of salt to taste.

❧

PLT (very little cutting required)

Cooking bacon is messy, and it's high in saturated fat; instead put 2–3 slices of Prosciutto in a dry pan over medium heat; turn after 2 minutes (or when lightly browned and curled), cook about 45 seconds longer. Spread a thin layer of mustard on lightly toasted whole wheat bread; spread the other slice with a 1/4 of an avocado, skinned; mash and spread with the back of a fork directly on the toast. Lay the Prosciutto on the bread slice with the mustard, top with sliced tomato, sprinkle with salt and pepper, then a large folded lettuce leaf. Top with avocado toast, press down firmly, then slice in half on the diagonal. **Variation**: Use 2 slices of Prosciutto and add a fried egg to the sandwich.

❧

Country Scramble

Heat a small skillet with 1 tsp. of butter over medium heat. Throw in a handful of frozen spinach, thawed and squeezed dry, or torn, fresh spinach, pinches of salt and pepper, and 1 or 2 eggs cracked right into the pan (watch for and remove pieces of the shell if needed). Scramble vigorously with a wooden spoon until just cooked (roughly 20-30 seconds); immediately plate. Serve with whole-wheat toast, corn tortilla, or inside a room temperature, lightly salted bell pepper half.

❧

RECIPES

Spinach and Potatoes with Feta (little or no cutting required)

For 2-4 servings, bake 2 white or sweet potatoes, or on your stovetop, simmer small new potatoes, barely covered with water, in a covered saucepan. Mix 1/4 cup each crumbled feta cheese and plain yogurt in a bowl. Stir in 2 Tbsp. dried (or chopped fresh) chives, 1/2 tsp. of salt, and a pinch each of cayenne and black pepper. Stir in 1/3 cup of frozen, thawed, and squeezed dry spinach. Let the mixture sit on the stovetop until the potatoes are cooked through. Spoon sauce over split and squeezed opened potatoes.

❧

Roasted Chickpeas

Soak 1 cup of dried chickpeas overnight in water to cover by about 2 inches. This will yield roughly 2 cups of soaked beans). Drain, rinse, and drain again. Spread in a single layer on a sheet pan and pat dry excess moisture. Sprinkle with 1/2 tsp. salt and 1/4 tsp. hot paprika or cayenne, or to taste. Bake in a preheated 300-degree oven for approximately 1-1/4 hours. Shake the pan a few times during this process and check for desired crunchiness after an hour. The drier they get, the tastier they are and the longer they'll store, but you'll want to protect your teeth and not get them too crunchy! Let dry completely before storing in an airtight container. You can use rinsed and drained canned chickpeas as well. The roasting time and temperature will be the same. Season to taste, but remember the canned will absorb more flavor from the seasonings than the dried beans.

❧

Trail Mix

For a homemade and less fat-intensive trail mix, combine roasted chickpeas with sliced or slivered almonds, currants (or small pieces of unsweetened dried fruit of your choice), and plain salted corn or rice cakes crumbled into popcorn-sized pieces. Add smaller amounts of pumpkin and sunflower seeds and walnut pieces. If using unsalted nuts and seeds, sprinkle the mixture with a bit of salt to taste, toss well. The salt will cling to the currants and produce a delightful salty-sweet combination of flavors. Store in an airtight container.

❧

Fran's Favorite Quinoa Clusters

On a parchment lined sheet pan, combine 3/4 cup quinoa, 2 Tbsp. sesame or sunflower seeds (or 1 Tbsp. each), 2-1/2 Tbsp. each of pumpkin seeds and maple syrup, and 1/8 tsp. salt. Mix well with your hands (or use a spoon) until the quinoa is coated. Spread out in a single layer and roast in a preheated 410-degree oven for 10–14 minutes, or until golden brown. Turn the sheet pan after 8 minutes and begin to watch carefully after 10; it will brown quickly towards the end. Allow to cool completely, break into clusters, and store in an airtight container.

Baked Bananas and Grapefruit (little cutting required)

Grease a baking dish and preheat the oven to 350 degrees. For 4 servings, cut 1 grapefruit (or 2 oranges) into segments; do this in a bowl so that you capture all the juices. Stir in 1/4 tsp. each cinnamon and nutmeg. Halve 2 bananas, lengthwise; keep fruit in the peel. Place each half, flesh side up, in the baking dish and drizzle them evenly with 1 Tbsp. of molasses. Pour the citrus and spices over the bananas and bake for 10-15 minutes. Serve bananas in their peel in dishes and spoon citrus and sauce over, and around, them.

Leftover Brown Rice Pudding

Combine 1-1/2 cups of cooked rice in a saucepan with about 3/4 cup of milk (enough to barely cover the rice), 1-1/2 Tbsp. maple syrup, 1/8 tsp. ea. of cinnamon, and cardamom or nutmeg, 1 Tbsp. plus 1 tsp. of currants or chopped dried apricots, and 1-1/2 tsp. ea. of pumpkin seeds or ch. almonds, and sesame seeds (if you have them on hand). Simmer over low heat, partially covered, until rice absorbs most, but not all, of the milk, approximately 7-10 minutes.

Leftover Savory Rice

For a quick savory use of left-over rice, melt one tsp. of butter and lightly scramble 1-2 eggs directly into a medium-sized sauté pan; remove to a small plate. Coat the bottom of the same saucepan with 2 Tbsp. of water and 1 Tbsp. plus 1 tsp. of soy sauce, and 1/8 tsp. salt. Bring to a simmer and immediately add 1-1/2 cups of left-over rice (or a package of plain pre-cooked brown rice), 1/2 cup ea. of frozen peas, corn, and spinach, 1/8 tsp. each of salt, 1/4 tsp. each cayenne and vinegar, and a half to a full small can of drained sliced water chestnuts (or use fresh bean sprouts instead, added the last minute of cooking time). Stir well from the bottom, cover, and decrease the heat to low for 2-3 minutes, or until hot. Uncover, and stir in the egg. Torn fresh basil or cilantro leaves, and snipped scallions or chives, added at the end, are excellent additions if you have them on hand.

∽

Mini Leftover Rice Cakes

I enjoy these so much that I will cook and cool down a batch of rice just to make them. They remind me of an Italian version of potato latkes. Toast 1 slice of whole wheat bread or a whole wheat pita; slightly cool and chop finely (you want 1/3 cup for this recipe). To 1-1/4 – 1-1/3 cups of cooked rice in a mixing bowl, add 1/2 cup grated Romano or Parmesan cheese, 1/4 cup each of chopped parsley and scallions (or minced onion), 1 finely chopped clove of garlic, 1/8 - 1/4 tsp. crushed red chiles, and 1/8 tsp. salt. Combine ingredients with a fork. Crack an egg on top, tip the bowl a bit, and scramble the egg with the fork against the side of the bowl; combine with the other ingredients. Add the bread crumbs and mix well with the fork. Shape into 8 small patties. Heat 1-1/2 tsp. of olive oil over medium heat and sauté in the hot oil for approximately 4 minutes on each side (flatten a bit with a spatula when you turn them over). When a golden-brown crust has formed on each side remove it to a serving plate and sprinkle with an additional 1/8 tsp. of salt, if desired, or to taste.

∽

Irio (Traditional Mashed Vegetable Dish from Kenya)

Before preparing, place an unopened 10 oz. package of frozen chopped spinach in a bowl filled with water to thaw. Cut 1 lb. of potatoes into 1/2" dice. Place in a saucepan with 1-1/2 cups of water. Bring to a boil, lower heat, and simmer slowly, partially covered, until just tender and most of the water has evaporated. Stir in

2/3 cup of frozen corn, 1 cup of frozen peas, and the squeezed dry spinach. Cover; turn off the heat after 1-1/2 minutes. Uncover and stir in 1/2 Tbsp. of butter, 1/2 tsp. salt, or to taste, and 1/8 tsp. pepper. Coarsely mash the vegetables together. Serve with small lemon wedges, if desired.

Crudité with Curry Dip

In a serving bowl, combine 1-1/2 tsp. each of curry powder and balsamic (or other) vinegar. Mix in 1-1/2 tsp. each of olive oil and honey (measure the oil first so the honey will slide right off the measuring spoon). Stir in 3/4 tsp. of salt and 3/4 cup of plain yogurt. This dip is great with every fresh vegetable I can think of, steamed artichokes, and also cold left-over cooked vegetables and chicken.

Canned Fish Plate

Open a can of sardines or canned fish of your choice. Lift fish out of the brine, or if packed in its own juices, stir them back into the fish; transfer to a serving dish. To the plate, add a few radishes or thin halved slices of raw onion (or both). Pour 1–2 capfuls of vinegar over all, and sprinkle with a pinch of salt. Add sour pickle relish (or slices or spears), and a few olives, alongside the fish on the plate, 1 celery stalk cut in quarters crosswise, 1 small bell pepper, quartered, seeded, lightly salted, and cut in half crosswise, and six lettuce leaves. Sprinkle fish and vegetables with ground pepper to taste. Use lettuce, pepper, and celery as "holders" for the rest of the ingredients. Rye crackers or rye bread make a good addition as well.

Easy Pumpkin Chili (little or no cutting required)

With a potato masher, partially crush 1–15 oz. can of rinsed and drained chickpeas directly into a medium-large saucepan. Add 1–15 oz. can each of pumpkin puree, diced tomatoes in juice, and pinto or kidney beans. Add 3 cans of water, 1/4 cup dried chives (or 1/3 cup fresh chopped chives or scallions), 1 Tbsp. chili powder, 2 tsp. each of salt and cumin, 1/4 tsp. black pepper, and 1 tsp. each of crushed red chiles, Tabasco, and oregano. Over medium-high heat, bring to boil, stirring occa-sionally. Lower heat and let simmer for approximately 25 minutes. If desired, serve with grated cheese and chopped onion, or chopped dry roasted peanuts and rice.

༄

Vegetable Eggdrop Soup (little or no cutting required)

For 2-3 servings, combine 2–15 oz. cans of chicken (or other) broth in a medium saucepan with salt and pepper to taste, 4-5 shakes of Tabasco, 1 tsp. each soy sauce, lemon or lime juice, and maple syrup, and 2 Tbsp. of dried (or chopped fresh) chives. Heat to boiling over medium-high heat. Meanwhile, crack 2 eggs into a bowl and scramble with a fork, leaving some of the egg not totally blended. When the mixture comes to a boil, add 1/3 cup each of frozen chopped spinach, peas, and corn (or 1-1/2 cups of cooked leftover vegetables, if you have any on hand in the refrigerator); simmer for 1 minute. Shut heat, and immediately, keep-ing the soup moving, stir in the egg gradually to form egg drops. If you have fresh bean sprouts, cilantro, basil, chile, fish sauce, lemon or lime wedges on hand, serve any or all of them with the soup.

༄

Jorge's Easy Lentil Soup (very little cutting required)

Bring 1/2 lb. (1-1/2 cups) of rinsed and picked through brown (or green) lentils, 6 cups of water, 1/2 tsp. salt, and 1/4 tsp. pepper, to a boil; simmer gently for approximately 1 hour, or until lentils are cooked through and beginning to disin-tegrate; simmer about 10-15 minutes longer. Add 1/2-3/4 tsp. salt to taste, the juice of 1/2 a lemon, 2-1/4 cups of torn or chopped spinach or mustard (or other leafy) greens. Bring back to a boil, stir soup vigorously, and crack in 4 room tem-perature eggs, one at a time; keep them separate and away from the edges of the pot. Keep the soup moving by stirring along the pot's perimeter to avoid touching the eggs. Lower heat; barely simmer the soup for 3-1/2 - 4 minutes. Turn off the heat. Ladle soup and 1 poached egg into each bowl, careful not to break the yolk. Serve with warm corn tortillas or crusty peasant bread (Jorge would hard-poach the eggs but I prefer the flavor and texture of the soup after the runny yolk melds into the broth).

～

Lemon Parmesan Romaine Salad (very little cutting required)

For 3 salad servings, cut or tear 8 cups of romaine lettuce leaves into 1" pieces. Drizzle with 2-1/4 Tbsp. of olive oil. Stir lettuce with a fork to coat all the pieces. Add 1/2 tsp. salt, 1/4 tsp. pepper, 1 minced clove of garlic, and 2 Tbsp. of lemon juice (approx. 1 lemon); stir to coat, and add 2/3 cup grated Romano or Parmesan. Toss to combine well, and serve. **Variation**: Partially mash or chop 6 anchovy fillets (or use anchovy paste); add to salad bowl with the oil, combining well; add the romaine, toss, and continue tossing in remaining ingredients, including homemade baked croutons, if desired. **Second Variation**: Toss the greens with the parmesan, salt, pepper, garlic, and 2 Tbsp. lemon juice, leaving out the oil. In a skillet over medium-low heat, add 6 anchovy fillets (from a jar or can), wiped of excess oil (but leave some oil) that adheres to them. Add 1-1/2 Tbsp. oil to the skillet and let anchovies soften for a minute or so; mash lightly. Blend in 2-1/2 Tbsp. water, 1 tsp. wine vinegar, and then crack open 3 eggs into the pan. Swirl pan gently, cover, lower heat, and cook for 1-1/2 minutes. Uncover; spread whites out a bit with a spatula, re-cover, and cook an additional minute, or until whites are set and yolks are still runny. With a spatula, carefully lift out and top each salad with one egg and a third of the anchovy sauce.

～

Kale Salad

Rinse and shake dry 1 large bunch of curly kale. Dry well with a clean kitchen towel and cut out the thick bottom stems; coarsely chop the kale to make 6 full cups. In a large serving bowl, whisk together 3 Tbsp. olive oil, 2 Tbsp. plus 1 tsp. lemon juice, 1 Tbsp. plus 1 tsp. tamari or soy sauce, 1/3 tsp. salt, and 1/4 tsp. pepper. Add the kale and toss to coat evenly. Add 1/2 a small red onion and 1 halved, seeded bell pepper, both sliced in half again lengthwise and sliced thinly crosswise, and 1/4 cup total of any combination of sunflower, pumpkin, and sesame seeds, or chopped nuts. This salad holds well for a few days in the refrigerator. You can top the salad with crumbled feta, queso Cotija, or cheese of your choice, for added depth of flavor and extra protein.

∽

Cabbage and Bean Salad

Rinse and drain 1 can each of chickpeas, and kidney beans or pintos. Shred 1/2 head of green cabbage and 1/4 of a small head of red cabbage. Thinly slice 1 small and halved red onion and 2 celery stalks. In a large serving bowl, whisk together 1/3 cup of olive oil and 1/4 cup red wine vinegar, 1/2 a bunch of chopped parsley, 3/4 tsp. of salt, and 1/4 tsp. each of ground black pepper and cayenne. Toss in the cabbage, onion, bell pepper, and beans; coat well with the dressing. This salad holds up for several days in the refrigerator.

Side Dishes

Cooking Dried Beans

Begin by sorting through them, discarding anything that's not a bean, rinse, and drain. Soaking beans overnight can make them easier to digest and decrease the cooking time by a bit. I don't find it necessary, but soak them if you prefer. Soaked or not, add 2 cups of uncooked beans to 8 cups of water (approximately 2" above the beans); stir in 1/4 tsp. of crushed chile flakes and 1/2 an onion, diced or just peeled. Bring to a boil, lower the heat, and cook (at a low boil) until just tender, replenishing with warm water as needed to keep the level a little over 1" above the beans; raise the heat as you stir in more water to bring it quickly back to a boil; then lower the heat and continue to cook the beans at a low boil. Cooking times will vary with the freshness of the dried beans, but most varieties cook within 1-1/4 - 1-3/4 hours after coming to a simmer. Black-eyed peas, adzuki, and other smaller beans take less time. For creamy beans, cover the pot while cooking. For separate and firmer beans, cook uncovered. Season the cooked beans with pepper and 2 tsp. of salt, or to taste.

Lentils with Coriander and Honey

Pick through, rinse, and drain the lentils. In a medium saucepan, over medium heat, combine 1 cup of lentils, 3 cups of water (about 1-1/2" above the lentils), 1 whole scallion or 1/4 peeled onion, and 1/2 tsp. each of salt and coriander. Bring to a boil, lower heat, and simmer, partially covered, for 30-50 minutes (check brown lentils after 20-25 minutes; green and French lentils will take longer). Remove the onion; sprinkle with an additional 1/4 tsp. each of salt and coriander, if desired. Stir in 1-1/2 – 2 cups of fresh roughly chopped or torn spinach or baby spinach, and 1 Tbsp. each of honey and olive oil. **Variation**: For a complete protein meal, serve the lentils with or over steamed rice. A crisp salad will add a wonderful texture to the meal.

Roasted Vegetables

I find the following vegetables lend themselves particularly well for roasting. Since many of them have different cooking times, I've specified cutting them at different sizes so they'll cook through at the same time in case you want to mix and match those vegetables. Otherwise, choose veggies that have similar time and size requirements (like most root vegetables), cut them whatever size you like (but not too big, or they'll burn before they cook through), and roast until they're al dente on the inside and crispy brown on the outside. You might need to lower the heat if they're browning too quickly. Selecting from vegetables you have on hand is a great way to clean out your refrigerator. Cut enough to fully cover, but not crowd, the bottom of a sheet pan. If vegetables are piled up or crowded they will steam rather than roast. Cut butternut squash, white and sweet potato, rutabaga, turnip, and *eggplant in 2/3 - 3/4" dice. Cut onion, carrots, and celery in 1-1/2" dice and red or green cabbage, bell pepper, and cauliflower into 2 - 2-1/4" pieces. Leave brussels sprouts, scallions, crimini or white mushrooms, and peeled garlic cloves whole (or cut in half if large), and slice summer squash in half crosswise. If you prefer cutting your summer squash into 1 - 1-1/2" slices or adding trimmed asparagus spears, add them (lightly oiled and salted) during the last 8-12 minutes, depending on their size. To begin: in a medium bowl, lightly coat roughly 4 cups of cut vegetables (plus halved squash, if using) with 2 tsp. olive oil and 1 tsp. each balsamic vinegar and lemon juice; sprinkle with 1/2 – 3/4 tsp. salt, and 1/4 tsp. each black pepper, thyme, and rosemary. Combine well, spread in a single layer on a sheet pan (parchment-lined will make clean-up easier), and roast in a preheated 445-degree oven for 20 minutes. Remove the pan from the oven. As quickly and as best as you can, move the vegetables along the outer edges to the middle of the pan with a spatula, and those in the middle to the outside edges. Remove any vegetables that are cooked and browned enough (you can replace them during the final minute of cooking to reheat). This would be a good time to add any quick-cooking additions. The other vegetables would have shrunken enough by then to push them a bit (without piling them) towards the center of the pan to make space around the perimeter if needed (or you can use another pan if you need more room). Turn the pan around, return it to the oven, and continue cooking for approximately 10 minutes more, or until the vegetables are done. *Eggplant will cook more quickly than the vegetables of the same size that I paired them with, but I prefer them cut that size so they'll dry out instead of getting mushy. **Variation**: To make **Potato Chips**, thinly slice off the bottom length of 1 russet potato so it will sit flat on your cutting board. Carefully slice the potato as thinly as you can while keeping the slices whole. Line a sheet pan with parchment. Grease the paper with olive oil. In a single layer, arrange the slices closely together, but not touching (put the thinnest slices in the center and the thicker ones along the edges). With oiled hands or a brush, lightly coat the tops of the slices. Bake in a preheated 350-degree oven until lightly brown at the edges (about 20 minutes). Flip over (or remove if done) the ones that are getting too brown. Bake 5–10 minutes longer, or until cooked through and crispy. Sprinkle evenly with 1/3 tsp. of salt. Allow to cool for several minutes before serving. Variation: Sprinkle with a small amount of cider or malt vinegar before salting.

Baked Corn Tortillas or Whole Wheat Pita Chips

Cut pita or tortillas in half, stacked two at a time; then cut each half into three wedges. For pita, open each wedge and separate the top from the bottom. Arrange in a single layer on a lightly greased sheet pan. Spray tops or brush lightly with extra virgin olive oil and sprinkle lightly with salt, or leave them plain without salt. Bake in a preheated 415-degree oven for approximately 6-8 minutes for pitas and 10-12 minutes for tortillas, or until crisp. Watch closely near the end of cooking time; they will brown quickly. Let cool for several minutes before serving.

Whole and Hulled Grains and Seeds

Oldways Whole Grains Council and Grains and Legumes Nutrition Council websites are excellent sources of nutritional information that include recipes for a wide variety of grains and legumes. Access to whole grains can be a challenge in many areas. Most health food stores will carry them, pre-packaged or in bulk. Conventional markets might carry some, and they may be able to help you locate a source for others. Like beans, soaking large grains overnight could make them easier to digest. Also like beans, you can prepare them by boiling them in generous amounts of water until desired tenderness is reached.

Pearled and polished grains have had their outer hull, bran, and germ removed. Semi-pearled (semi-perlato) grains have had the hull and part of the bran and germ removed. Hulled grains, also known as groats when cracked, have had only the tough inedible outer hull removed. The latter takes longer to cook but contains more fiber and overall nutritional value, and typically has a more nutty flavor and chewy texture.

Note: Following recipes that call for a slow steaming simmer, rather than boiling the grains, can be tricky; variations in "low" stovetop settings, the material and thickness of the pan used, and the seal you get from its lid, play major roles in the outcome. Adjustments might need to be made, especially when preparing a recipe for the first time. Be ready to pour or boil away excess liquid, or to add more liquid, bring quickly back to a simmer, cover, and adjust the cooking time.

෨

Bulgur

To prepare bulgur (cracked parboiled whole wheat berries), bring 1-1/4 cups of water to a boil, stir in 1 cup bulgur, cover tightly, and turn off the heat right away. Leave the pan on the hot burner for 25 minutes. The water should be absorbed fully; drain if any remains. Fluff with a fork while mixing in 1 tsp. olive oil and 1/2 tsp. salt. **Variation**: measure 1 cup of bulgur into a heatproof serving bowl with a tight-fitting lid. Bring 1-1/4 cups of water to a boil; pour over the bulgur, stir, and cover right away. Let sit on your warm stovetop for 25 minutes until done. Meanwhile, sauté 1/2 a diced onion and 6 diced mushrooms in 1-1/2 tsp. butter or oil and 1/2 tsp. salt over medium-low heat for about 8 minutes; stir into the soaked bulgur and serve. **Second Variation**: For a delicious **Tabouli** salad, coat the soaked bulgur with 3-4 Tbsp. olive oil. Add 1/3 cup each of fresh finely chopped green onions and mint (if you can't find fresh mint, add additional parsley and green onion in its place), 1-1/2 cups of finely chopped parsley, 1/2 tsp. salt, 1/4 tsp. black pepper, and 3-4 Tbsp. lemon juice. Stir in 2 fresh finely chopped tomatoes before serving and add salt to taste. Serve with romaine lettuce leaves to scoop up the tabouli.

Quinoa

Rinse and drain 1/2 cup of quinoa. Sauté 1/2 a small chopped onion in 1-1/4 tsp. olive oil or butter in a small saucepan over medium heat for 2 minutes. Add 1/3 tsp. salt; add quinoa and stir to coat with the onion and oil. Add 1/2 cup each of water and orange juice; bring to a simmer. Cover the pan and cook over low heat for 15 minutes. Shut the fire and let rest on the hot burner for 5 minutes. Fluff with a fork and serve.

Brown Rice

For approximately 3 cups of cooked rice, bring 10 cups of water to a boil (the ratio is 10 cups per 1 cup of rice). Meanwhile, rinse 1 cup of brown Basmati or Jasmine rice (these long-grain types are less starchy and I prefer their flavor and texture, but you can cook any variety you like) in a strainer for a half minute or so. When water comes to a boil, stir in the rice. Adjust the heat so that the water stays at a moderate boil. Drain after 29-30 minutes; return to the pot, cover tightly, and allow the rice to steam in the moisture still clinging to it, on the hot but turned off burner, for 8-10 minutes. With a fork, fluff rice while mixing in 1 tsp. butter and 1/3 tsp. salt, or to taste. **Variation**: For a **brown and white rice combination**, use 2/3 cup of rinsed brown rice instead of 1 cup. After adding to the boiling water, rinse 1/3 cup of white rice in the same strainer (or use a 1/2 cup of each). After the brown rice has been cooking for 14 minutes, raise the heat and slowly stir in the white rice (so you don't lose the boil). Lower heat to keep at a moderate boil and cook for 15 minutes. Drain, transfer back to the pot, cover, and finish as directed above.

∾

Wheat Berries (Farro, Emmer, Einkorn, *Spelt)

Sauté 1/2 a chopped onion and 6 diced mushrooms slowly over medium-low heat in 1 tsp. each of olive oil and butter, with 1/3 tsp. salt and 1/8 tsp. black pepper until the onion browns. Add 3/4 cup of rinsed and drained wheat berries. Stir to coat with the onion and oil for 2-3 minutes. Add 2-1/4 cups of water, raise the heat, bring to a boil, cover, lower heat, and simmer gently for 45 minutes (30 minutes, if using pearled). Uncover, raise the heat, and simmer for 10-15 minutes, stirring occasionally, until most of the liquid has evaporated.

During the last minute or two, stir in 2 or 3 handfuls of torn or baby spinach or chopped leafy greens and 1/2 tsp. lemon juice. Cover, cook for 1 minute, uncover, season to taste, and serve. If there are any leftovers, I often make a hearty "barley" type soup with them the next day by adding beef broth, sliced carrots and celery, salt, pepper, and thyme; simmer until the carrots and celery are just cooked. Finish with a squeeze of lemon. Kamut is a brand name for Khorasan wheat berries. It has a slightly larger grain and a golden quality to its light brown coloring. When preparing **Kamut** or ***Spelt**: to the above recipe, add an additional 1/2 cup of water and increase the covered cooking time by 15 minutes. I find spelt has a chewier texture than the other wheat berries and I'm particularly fond of using it as the star ingredient in a salad.

∾

Breakfast Amaranth and Millet

Bring 1/2 cup of millet and 1-1/2 cups of water to a boil with 1/6 tsp. salt; simmer, covered, for 15 minutes. Raise the heat, add 1/2 cup of amaranth and 1 cup of room temperature water; bring to a boil quickly, lower the heat, and gently simmer, covered, for another 15 minutes. Enjoy fresh with a little butter and honey or maple syrup, or for the following day's breakfast, pour into a greased loaf pan while hot, cool it down, cover, and refrigerate. Approximately 15 minutes before serving, cut slices about 3/4" thick and sauté over medium-high heat in a little butter until heated through and golden brown on both sides; serve with honey or maple syrup, or with a fried egg on top.

Whole Wheat Couscous

I've never seen the larger round grains available in whole wheat, but for small grain couscous, bring 1-1/3 cups of water to a boil in a medium saucepan with 2 tsp. of olive oil and 1/2 tsp. of salt. Shut fire and remove from heat; stir in 1 cup of couscous. Cover and let sit for 6-8 minutes. Fluff in 2 tsp. of butter with a fork, and serve.

CHAPTER 10

Conclusion

A few years ago, I returned from a trip to Portugal and Spain where I spent a month in southern Portugal building a tiny earthen "cob" studio with an exciting group of people, mostly young adults from around the world. Cob houses are built from damp mixtures of clay soil, sand, and straw; they are molded to form, left to partially dry, and then trimmed before subsequent layers are applied. They particularly interest me as a Californian because these strong structures are fireproof. The typical thick wall construction provides excellent thermal mass insulation, creating an environment easy to keep cool in the summer and warm in the winter. Builders do not require power tools to construct simple structures and their material costs remain low and void of hazardous waste; however, they are labor-intensive. Although cob buildings can be found in many areas across the globe, some still standing after centuries, most planning departments in the United States have no existing building codes for cob dwelling approval.

To rest after such a strenuous task, I made my way to Seville for two weeks. As a chef, I've always dreamt of experiencing the "tapas bar culture" found throughout Spain. Although one can order full-size portions, tapas bars primarily serve "small plates," along with beer and wine. Their small portions are usually substantial, and in my experience, two dishes can satisfy even a large appetite like mine. Since their prices reflect the small portion sizes, eating at a tapas bar provides both an affordable meal and a way to sample a variety of dishes rather than just one. While some items can be expensive, the tapas menus I saw always contained ample offerings that cost little, like small bowls of marinated lupini beans, olives, peanuts in the shell, and marinated or grilled vegetables, croquetas, or a wedge of their famous "Omelet Espagnol"; some tapas bars provide the beans, olives or nuts gratis with a drink order. I often discovered tapas bars situated together near small playgrounds with tables and chairs set up outside so the adults could chat while the children played. And one particular square I often passed featured a radio and speakers that played swing tunes so that people could dance throughout the evening. To me, this food culture epitomizes what I love about the community of the table. This style of eating also provides a good exercise in restraint. When I did join others at a tapas bar, the sharing of plates called for awareness that everyone deserved their share; this attention to the needs of others encouraged savoring over devouring.

Traveling alone has its advantages, but also its drawbacks, and the tapas bar culture called attention to the latter. Watching other people have fun and socialize around me in a language I could hardly speak was less than ideal. Perhaps, because of my experience, I would add to this beautiful way of eating a "singles" table set aside for people on their own, so they might meet new people and socialize. I think that such an idea could work in restaurants in the United States as well. As a single woman who loves to converse over a meal, being able to spontaneously join others at a convivial table would lead me to dine out more often. When I traveled in Germany and France with Geoff many years ago, we often found ourselves seated with others in a crowded restaurant. The people we joined didn't seem to feel possessive about "their space," as people in the United States might. To change this aspect of our food culture, restaurants here might create a "social section," akin to the smoking and non-smoking sections of the past. Customers could choose whether they want to sit in the "social section" or the "do not disturb" (unless you're my waitperson) section. Done gradually, starting with small social sections of one or two tables to test the waters, this concept might prove successful for both customers and restaurants, who might see increased revenue through maximizing more of their seating capacity.

This tapas culture also creates lively streets at night. People were out and about, often until midnight when the street cleaners would take their place. I've seen a similar night culture in Mexico, where families come out in the evening to enjoy street food and music. When people, including families with children, use the streets at night, those streets typically become much safer. In all of my travels, I must sadly admit that I've felt the least safe walking around after dark in my own country.

Travel, even when locally created, not only provides exposure to local foods and different peoples, but it allows for the exchange of ideas between one culture and another. I hope that one day soon the study of U.S. and world history and geography in our primary and secondary schools will be expanded and refined, structured around the evolution of a population's living conditions, their cuisine (of course), their art, music, and dance, their natural landscapes, and wildlife. Students could, when possible, connect online with students from the countries being studied, learning first a limited foreign vocabulary. In this way, the other members of our global community might cease to be strangers. This system could also work well used among students of different ethnic backgrounds and walks of life here in our own country.

This style of learning about our world can connect disparate cultures by revealing the common challenges and triumphs that unite us, helping us to overcome the "fear of the other" that now divides us. We have so much to learn from one another. If we could study and identify the most just, beneficial, and successful elements of each culture on this planet and integrate these elements into the best aspects of our cultural heritage, we would enjoy a more fulfilling society. Insisting on the superiority of individual cultures and countries makes it impossible to acknowledge that we all have something of value to bring to a welcoming table. Progress in our own country will only begin when we stop wasting our time trying to change people's minds and belittling them because of their differing views. We don't need to always agree with each other, but we do need to get along and accept our differences. Dismissing other people as ignorant, arrogant, appalling, absurd, or rude only drives us further apart.

Instead, we should try to create solutions to the problems we share based on our common ground, always remembering that we can all act in unproductive and foolish ways, especially when we isolate ourselves from others. One doesn't have to believe that people have contributed to climate change to support less toxic conditions on our planet; people can oppose affirmative action and still want to end the deeply ingrained racial, gender, and economic inequality in this country; one can protest against Israel's treatment of Palestinians without hating Jews, just as Jews can work for Israel to end those subjugating policies while the government keeps its focus on the safety of their citizens. One needn't be pro-immigration to object to the treatment of the refugees at our southern border and those held in detention centers throughout the country; one can support "tough on crime" policies and still work for prison, policing, and justice reform; people opposed to legalized abortion and those who support choice can nonetheless work together to reduce the number of abortions by supporting measures to improve conditions for low-income and single women who use that service the most. People who don't own guns and those who do can stand resolutely together until we have responsible gun ownership measures secured alongside our right to bear arms; proponents of a contracted government can combine forces with those in favor of its expansion to work on improving the quality of government (reducing waste, redundancy, and corruption would automatically reduce its size and expenditures). Having a Neighborhood Café inside the Capitol Building, for representatives only, might allow our lawmakers to clean their own house by providing a genial space, free from lobbyists and reporters, in which to unleash their imaginations. And all around the world, genuine patriots can love their countries while still trying to make them better. If we fail to get beyond the "my side, your side" mentality, we will remain vulnerable to the forces implementing their intimidating vision of the world while we remain distractedly nitpicking and bickering amongst ourselves. Creating a plan based on our commonalities to forward our vision for a more just society while enjoying good food and friendly social interaction defines the purpose of a Neighborhood Café.

We don't need to be experts in a subject to have a helpful opinion, and making decisions by integrating common sense and ethics from all sides of an argument can help transform our society. Yet how can we create such conversations until we learn how to act thoughtfully in our public sphere and refrain from reacting wildly and judgmentally? Analyzing verified information, weighing its pros and cons, practicing the art of debate, striving to collaborate and compromise, and allowing the majority to prevail - this epitomizes democratic living.

Compromise is an artistic activity and a show of strength, not weakness. Reducing the craft to a win/lose interpretation doesn't allow for the recognition of how hard it is to give up something one cares deeply about for the common good. When such acts go unappreciated, it sours the entire process and negatively impacts future opportunities.

When most of us come to our own conclusions, guided by our sense of fairness, humor for our common human condition, and gratitude for what we already have, I have no doubt society will evolve ethically. Too often our national and global politics and media outlets frustrate progress, justice, and equality by keeping the public too busy, tired, cynical, ill-informed, divided, or discouraged to strive towards positive change. But we can overcome such obstacles, and a Neighborhood Café can help support this process.

I'm not naive: I don't believe that simply changing our thoughts and behaviors will result in the positive changes we want to see in our society, particularly because such personal transformations do not occur easily. However, they define the starting point for building a healthy environment from which to confront our challenges. Creating an infrastructure that benefits both business and people, and forging relationships between people of differing colors, faiths, perspectives and economic positions, are no easy tasks. Additionally, the minority that currently benefits from and dictates the inequality of our economic systems will do everything in their power to keep us divided and distracted. Yet many powerful political and business leaders want meaningful social and economic change as well, and likely more would join such a movement as they observe positive changes unfolding. When we look at things impartially, we have the intelligence to see through bad actors, and we have the tenacity to stay strong and committed to our ideals.

Solutions to our most pressing problems are rarely black or white; their complexities can easily shut us down, curb our desire to proceed, and lead to the formulation of rash and counterproductive opinions. I certainly indulged in such unproductive behaviors until writing this book forced me to research all sides of particular issues. I've found the writing of this book an exasperating process, especially since one complex question always seems to lead to another, but I've also found the process exhilarating and empowering. Most questions led me to the same place, an understanding that "natural" isn't always best and big business and technology aren't always menacing - that genuine social progress can only be made when we harness the latter two to the goal of protecting human rights and the welfare of our planet. Innovation is crucial to our evolution; however, we must resist the present system that favors innovation, maximum production, and short-term profits over our moral charge to protect our planet and each other's well-being.

Short-term perspectives are typically borne out of our preoccupation with the present. The "Be Here Now" philosophy my generation grew up with was insightful and significant, but it was also flawed. As important as it is to live in the moment, it cannot exclude the responsibility we have to preserve our future for the generations to come.

Perhaps you think it's hopeless, that change at this point is impossible; it's easy enough to feel that way at times. For example, why waste our time trying to stop the use of one hazardous chemical only to have it replaced with another? However, that is also a coherent argument for transitioning to a lasting organic agricultural landscape. Perhaps you think you know all of this already, but still doubt that you can make a difference. Besides, you're too busy, too much in need of relaxation, and have no time for ideas that have little to do with your daily life and struggle to support your family. I can surely understand that feeling; I find it hard enough to leave at night once I'm home and relaxed for the evening or get up early on a weekend morning, even for things I love to do. As a single working mom, I paid little heed to political concerns except at election time, when I insisted on voting. We can all just do what we can. If voting, remaining open-minded, friendly, and committed to starving negativity represents all we can do, that's significant. Perhaps it will be our young and retired populations, or those who see peaceful activism as a new family activity, who will take us even further in the direction of deeper change. As long as people engage with questions of social responsibility in a cooperative, constructive way we won't be abdicating our power to those who now drive our government in a destructive direction. As we work together towards positive change and begin to diffuse much of the anger that has taken its toll on our country, we must keep our focus on correction, not punishment or revenge.

Rather than allowing "the system" to manipulate us, we must learn to do the manipulating by transforming the way we look at ourselves and our development. All of us live within the context of our social and cultural frameworks, but we must learn to critique those systems and look outside of them. Although a great country in many respects, the United States in the first decades of the twenty-first century remains a nation of extreme wealth and even more extreme poverty, of drug, electronic, and food addictions, characterized by widespread disdain for others, depression, and violence. As a society, we face many complex problems and challenges, but sometimes implementing just one simple change can lead to other changes, can initiate a cascade of changes. Although my vision of the Neighborhood Café addresses many issues, it focuses largely on the importance of clean, healthy food. Progress towards achieving a single goal – designing a public space where people can eat healthful foods and discuss in a constructive fashion possible solutions to the problems that beset us – can, however, lead to a less polluted and more unified planet. It can lower health care costs because we'll be a healthier population, create good jobs, better working conditions for many people, perhaps less demand for drugs, human trafficking, or the need to migrate; perhaps it can help form more empowered and engaged citizens. Attending to one issue, like healthy food, expands in the doing and can lead to so much more; but everything begins with the individual, with us, with our assumptions, attitudes, tolerances, and choices, which we have the power to change.

Stress probably causes more illness than any other factor in our lives, even a poor diet, and conflict between peoples causes a great deal of the stress that afflicts us. We would all benefit from becoming more adept at listening to and communicating with others, separating people from their beliefs, condemning actions rather than individuals, and competing or disagreeing freely with respect, comic relief, and genuine regard.

There's nothing I dislike more than the mistreatment of other living beings, the bullying and pitting of people against each other that is fast overtaking social and political discourse in this country. I remember as a girl visiting my grandparents' home in Brooklyn for dinner almost every other Sunday. After dinner, when the bowls of whole nuts in their shells, nutcrackers, and dried fruit would come out, some of our political conversations would become heated. At times, to express a differing perspective more vehemently, the adults would get up from their seats and bang their hands on the table to make a point. Often at those moments my grandma Ida would rush in from the kitchen to try and calm everyone down.

I feel a lot like my grandma: I want people to get along. In my family, "not getting along" always came from a position of love, and my memories of those lively encounters remain happy ones. I find it deeply disturbing and sad to see how often "not getting along" today creates unloving, uncaring, and toxic judgmental environments. Can we find the courage it will take to change these hostile environments in an age when people often shame, mock, and criticize sincerity and good intentions? I hope so, because we're not the cause of each other's problems, but the way out of them. I believe that this heartfelt, purposeful position defines the Neighborhood Café, which can provide a haven from which to explore our unrecognized potential, express our best selves, and build consensus on that foundation.

This represents my moral view of our evolution, of an ecologically-sound planet and a healthy food supply, in which diverse peoples live amicably, working together and thriving. Do enough of us wish for a better-functioning, kinder, more just, and healthier place to live? I believe so. Do too many of us wait for that technological breakthrough that will save us and the planet from the consequences of our actions? Do too many of us wait for a great leader to come along and solve our problems for us? While scientific advancements and exceptional leaders may help considerably, the most meaningful changes come from us. The long-term changes we control are the internal ones we cultivate within us, and as long as we keep doing that work, we will always have that great leader, hero, and role model we seek - in ourselves. None of us are perfect. If I could take back all the times in my life I behaved badly I would, but we don't get to do that. We get to move on, hoping to do better the next time. Most of us slog through life, doing the best with what we have; this demands much more and much harder work than the restaurant business. Instead of simply trudging distractedly or discouragingly onward, why not strive to imagine some place we really want to go. What describes your long-term vision for your life, your community, your country, your home planet? Perhaps A Neighborhood Café can help you formulate and attain that reality.

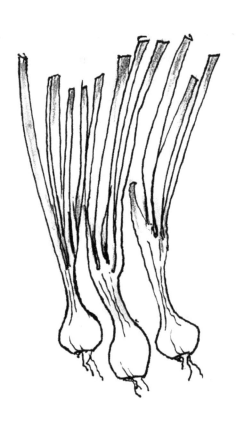

To Potential Customers of a
Neighborhood Café

This book advances my vision for "A Neighborhood Café," and I would be thrilled to see Neighborhood Cafés open in many neighborhoods and schools throughout our nation, indeed, throughout our world. However, even if a much more modest vision of such a success became reality, I would still be pleased. Yet for this to occur, potential customers of a Neighborhood Café would have to assume at least some responsibility, for only you can assure that those businesses meet the original intent of bringing healthy, tasty food and constructive information to the public, to you. If in doubt about a particular Neighborhood Café, asking to see their food storage area, or their most recent food invoices to check that they're using the nourishing ingredients they claim, would be reasonable requests, as well as asking for the sources of the information they offer. Make your assessment of those sources and the probity of the business as a whole. This, after all, defines the subject of this book: life represents a journey that must continually hone our belief in ourselves, in others, and in our power of discernment.

Acknowledgments

It is my good fortune to have a retired English Literature professor as a brother - Harold Weber. His work on this manuscript has given me a deep respect for the art of editing. I would send my finished chapters to him and he would return them transformed, fluidly expressing my thoughts, having changed and re-positioned words like a magician. As well, his council helped me stay on point throughout the writing of this book, and that was no easy task. Harold taught me to be a better writer. I remain indebted to him for his part in making my dream a reality.

Also instrumental in helping me bring this book to fruition is Christine McGlasson, my Marketing and Public Relations Consultant. She did so much more than what her title suggests. Chris helped me every step of the way, guiding me through these last four years with her expertise in so many book-related matters, and providing encouragement borne out of her total commitment to and belief in this project. She has become a dear friend in the process.

My other brother, Philip Weber, is a retired fine woodworker. Although not a photographer by trade, he possesses an artist's eye and talent. I am deeply grateful for the food photographs he took of many of the recipes found in this book. He endured several obstacles in the 2-1/2 weeks we had in Pensacola to get the task done. Working outside in the 100 degree Floridian summer heat because we lacked professional lighting equipment, and receiving help only from his sister, inexperienced in the art of food styling, were only two of the challenges he faced.

I want to thank my friend Linda Doerflinger for her insightful opinions, corrections, and probing questions that helped me to define my vision more clearly. I am grateful to my daughter-in-law, Valerie Oliver, for her extensive work in preparing and evaluating most of the recipes in this book, and my friend Carol Streib, who tested and commented on a number of "early draft" recipes, my aunt, Sylvia Weber, a career nurse, for confirming nutritional information in Chapters Four and Six, and to Dr. Deborah Angersbach for helping me come to understand some of the many complexities of nutritional science. I thank Ferndale dairyman and friend, Jim Regli, who offered his "inside" knowledge of organic and cooperative infrastructures, and Miriam Elizondo, whose computer assistance and friendly demeanor proved invaluable.

Seeing my vision of A Neighborhood Café come alive in a material form was an enjoyable process only because I had the help of two extremely gifted and delightful people. Carla Green of Clarity Designworks not only designed the cover, but artistically generated the files that laid out the interior formatting and translated my manuscript into a digital and print-ready book. She also helped me navigate my way through the intricate world of book publishing and distribution. Donna Bishop, responsible for the beautiful cover and interior illustrations, patiently extended her time to translate my vision onto paper.

Writing A Neighborhood Café has been a labor of love and a family affair in many ways. I am thus honored.

Recipe Index

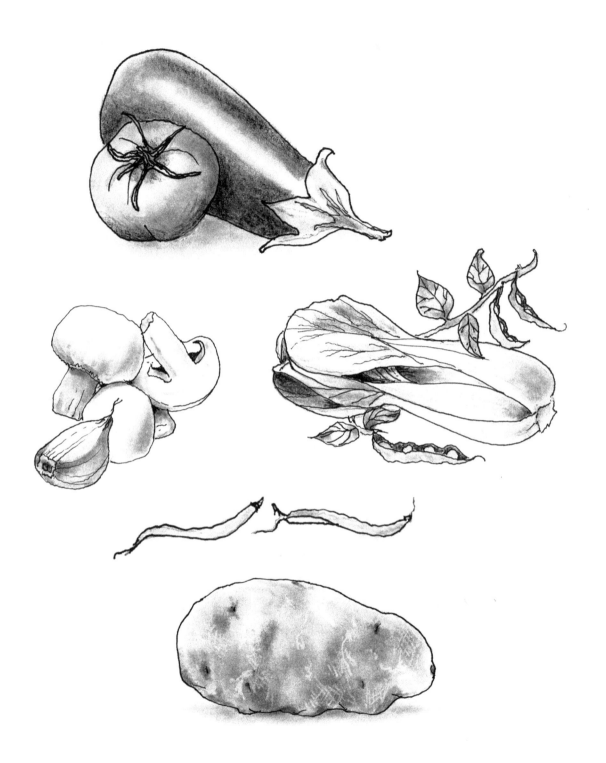